BookCaps Presents:

Les Misérables

In Plain and Simple English

Study Guide

BOOKCAPS

BookCaps™ Study Guides

www.bookcaps.com

Table of Contents

Historical Context

Les Miserables was published in Paris in 1862, written by Victor Hugo, and considered by most to be his masterpiece. Outside of France, Hugo is held in high esteem for his novels, in his native country, his poetry is also held in very high regard.

Victor Hugo was born in Besancon, in eastern France, in 1802, the third and youngest of the three illegitimate sons of Joseph Leopold Sigisbert Hugo and Sophie Trebuchet. His father was a career officer in Napoleon Bonaparte's army but his mother is considered a Royalist. As a writer, Hugo was able to draw upon his experiences with both factions and indeed, both sides are presented in *Les Miserables*, in accurate detail. One of Hugo's literary devices was to write long explanations of historical, social, and philosophical changes in France, particularly for the nineteenth century.

Hugo was born only three years after the period of the French Revolution ended. As a child growing up and even into his young adulthood, this period would be fresh in the minds of his elders and of course, had great influence on the changes brought by the Napoleonic period. The French monarchy, which had ruled absolutely for many centuries, crumbled and was destroyed within a few years. No other major power in Europe had gone through such a change and in fact, most of the changes enjoyed (or deplored) by other powers were more gradual and as in the case of Britain, through constitutional change that curbed the power of the monarch, which in effect avoided violent overthrow of the institution itself. Most of the novel, including flashbacks that lead at times to the novel's somewhat awkward construction, mostly covers the period between 1815 and 1834. There is an important reference to the Battle of Waterloo and a detailed analysis of the battle itself. The events of the battle lead to the "meeting" of two characters – the father of Marius Pontmercy and M. Thenardier.

During the same year as the Battle of Waterloo, 1815, the novel begins, the setting a small town in a remote area. It is here that the reader meets the protagonist of the story, Jean Valjean. Valjean represents the historical poor of the France of his day – the day to day struggle to avoid starvation and find shelter, the harsh inequities of the justice system, and the lingering influence of the Roman Catholic Church. He also plays a part in the uprising of 1832, which Hugo deftly describes, admirably capturing the mood of the times so that 21st century readers can vividly see, hear, and vicariously experience the passions and tribulations of the insurgents.

Hugo relates some of the history of France after Valjean's time as well, including an affectionate look at Louis-Philippe, who ruled as King of France from 1830-1848. He knew Louis-Philippe personally, but had no compunction about using the 1832 uprising as focal point of the novel.

Hugo prospered under Louis-Philippe, being made a life peer and member of the Upper House in 1845, but after the 1848 revolution deposed Louis-Philippe, Hugo went into exile, spending his final days as near to France as possible, on the Channel Islands, which are British Crown Dependencies. He died on the island of Guernsey in 1885.

Plot overview

Volume 1 introduces the reader to Jean Valjean, who has been released from imprisonment after serving nineteen years for the theft of a loaf of bread (with time added for bad behavior). He is given food and shelter by the local bishop of Digne. He steals from the bishop and is caught. The bishop allows him to go free but he steals again, this time from a child. He has a religious conversion and vows to turn his life around. Under an assumed name he goes to Montreuil-sur-Mer where he establishes a successful business and the town prospers. A native of the town, Fantine, returns. She has left her illegitimate daughter to be cared for in Montfermeil. Valjean promises to retrieve her daughter for her but fails to do so before she dies. Meanwhile, another man is being tried in his name – Valjean tells the judge that he is the real Valjean, returns to Montreuil-sur-Mer, and the policeman Javert arrests him, but allowing him time to retrieve Cosette, Fantine's daughter.

In Volume 2, Valjean is found and tried for his crimes. He is placed on a galley ship but escapes when saving another man's life. He heads to Montfermeil, to find Fantine's little girl, Cosette, now eight years old. She has been under the care of the Thenardiers, a despicable couple, who have two daughters about her age. They run an inn and are using Cosette for unpaid labor. Valjean, not revealing his identity, buys the girl from the Thenardiers. Valjean takes her to Paris, where they live in a run-down hovel but it is not long before Javert finds him. Valjean escapes with Cosette to a convent.

In Volume 3, the narrative moves forward a numbers of years.
Valjean and Cosette spend a few quiet years at the convent. The
reader is introduced to Marius Pontmercy, the son of a man who was
saved by Thenardier during the Battle of Waterloo. Marius has been
brought up by his grandfather, a royalist who hates Marius's father.
Marius is now studying law in Paris and living in the same building
as the Thenardier family now going by the name of Jondrette.
Marius is something of a loner and on his walks to the Luxembourg
gardens, he sees Cosette, who regularly visits with Valjean, now
known as M. Fauchelevent. Marius falls in love with her. The
Jondrettes, along with a gang known as the Patron-Minette, hatch a
plan to extort money from Valjean. Marius, looking through a
peephole from his room, sees Valjean and Cosette. The gang's plans
go awry and Javert arrests them but not before Valjean escapes
through the Jondrettes' window.

In Volume 4, Marius has discovered where Cosette lives, and dares
to speak to her as she sits in their garden alone. They declare their
love for each other. Eponine, the elder daughter of the Thenardier-
Jondrettes, knows the Patron-Minette gang have escaped from jail
and are after Valjean. She secretly lets him know and he decides to
take Cosette to England. Marius finds out about this and is broken-
hearted. He goes to the barricade in Rue de la Chanvrerie, where his
friends are leading an insurrection, and joins it. Eponine dies in the
onslaught, confessing her love for Marius. Gavroche, her brother
who has been estranged from his family for years, also dies.

In Volume 5 the uprising continues and the insurgents must admit defeat. Valjean and Marius, who is near death, escape into the sewer system. They come close to being captured by the police and reach the end of the line only to meet Thenardier who, after taking everything they have, unlocks the sewer grate to exit at the river's edge. He knows Javert is in the area, and the policeman captures Valjean and Marius. Javert is conflicted because Valjean had saved his life earlier at the barricades. He goes with the two men to Marius's grandfather's house and then leaves, only to commit suicide later. Marius and Cosette are reunited and marry. Marius has never been easy with Valjean, believing him to be a police spy. He does not know that Valjean saved his life. In time there is some estrangement between Cosette and Valjean which leads to Valjean's death, although not before Marius realizes what a good man he is and that he is the man who saved his life in the sewers of Paris.

Settings

The Bishop of Digne's residence

The bishop has transformed the residence from a palace of opulence to a place that he can treat the sick and give shelter to the poor. It is the first place Valjean finds refuge and from where he steals the bishop's silver – from this the story and action is plotted.

Montreuil-sur-Mer

This small city is where Valjean makes restitution for his crime of stealing from the bishop and from Little Gervais. He transforms it from a poor town to a thriving one where the residents are prosperous and happy. The loss of the town of Valjean leads to its downfall. It is also the hometown of Fantine, the doomed mother of Cosette.

Montfermeil

A small town where Fantine, on her way home to Montreuil-sur-Mer left her daughter in the care of the inn-keeper Thenardier and his wife. After her death, Cosette remains there until rescued by Valjean.

The Barricade, the Rue de la Chanvrerie, Paris

This small barricaded area is where the insurgents hold up for several days fighting the forces of authority: the National Guard and the army. It is where many of the minor but important characters die, such as M. Mabeuf, Eponine, Enjolras, and Gavroche.

The residence of M. Gillenormand

M. Gillenormand, the grandfather of Marius, gives the grandson and his bride Cosette, a place to live after the young man has recovered from his injuries suffering during the uprising. It is also where Valjean suffers the estrangement from Cosette that ultimately kills him.

Themes

Hidden Identity

The theme of hidden identity prevails throughout the novel. It begins with Jean Valjean being rejected in the public places of Digne due to his identity – his passport reveals that he is an ex-convict. From then on he rarely reveals his true identity, except when another man, Champmathieu, is assumed to be him. The Thenardiers also take on a false identity later in the book as a result of criminal activity. In one way or the other, a hidden or false identity works hand in hand with another theme – survival.

Survival

The struggle for survival is a theme found throughout *Les Miserables*. From a very early age Jean Valjean must use his wits just to get by. It is his action of stealing a loaf of bread to feed his starving nieces and nephews that sends him to the galleys for nineteen years. On his return to society he struggles for the next twenty years in one way or another, to live, to be accepted in society, and to live with his own conscience. Other characters also struggle in their own ways, both legal and illegal.

Religion

Roman Catholicism and faith play a large part in the novel, as they did in nineteenth century France. Two settings are religious in nature – the bishop's residence and the convent where Valjean and Cosette live quietly for a few years. The latter is a place of sanctuary for the two and their lives there are not included in the narrative. At the end of his life Valjean buys a crucifix for his wall, to be near him as he dies.

Interconnected lives

The interwoven lives of the characters reflect Hugo's motif of destiny in the novel. Valjean's life after he leaves the galleys is linked with several characters – Cosette, Javert, Fauchelevent, and the Thenardiers, to name a few. Marius also link to others – Thenardier, Eponine, Gavroche and ultimately Valjean. Hugo uses this device to combine the threads of the story.

Authority

Authority figures abound in *Les Miserables*, from the Bishop of Digne to the Judge in Champmathieu's trial, to the National Guard and the army, and of course, to M. Javert, the policeman who haunts Valjean for most of the novel. In the end his authority comes to naught as he lets Valjean go and then commits suicide. Authority has controlled Valjean's life, and finally, it indirectly leads to his death.

The Class System

Nineteenth century France was still governed by a class system even though some years have passed since the French Revolution. Hugo vividly describes the poor of Paris, both their deep melancholy and their *joie de vivre*. Try as they might, they can rarely become what they were not born into. Even Cosette, who goes from abject poverty to wealth, will never know her true background or she will lose everything, as Valjean does in the end.

Youth

The theme of youth is also common in *Les Miserables* and is often partnered with innocence as its main attribute. Examples of this include Fantine (during her relationship with Tholomyes), the Thenardier children (all five of them), Cosette, and Marius. In their own way, each of these individuals is innocent or the victims of circumstances and yet has the idealism of youth and light-heartedness. All of them are victims of their circumstances. Hugo explains the callousness of youth as simply a natural attribute.

Corruption and Villainy

The author does not condone corruption and villainy but in the case of the poor, he is forgiving. He is less kind to those with wealth or power who are corrupt, such as Javert and Gillenormand. Committing crime to survive is not nearly as heinous and treating people badly.

Gardens

The gardens of *Les Miserables* are the closest Hugo comes to having a motif or theme of nature. Various gardens, tended by Bishop Myriel, M. Mabeuf, Fauchelevent, and Marius's father Georges represent an escape from the harsh world – to create something beautiful in a harsh world. In the Luxembourg Garden and the garden of Cosette's home, Marius and Cosette discover their love for each other – it is allowed to blossom in the peaceful oasis of a garden.

Historical Context

Hugo often "breaks into" his story to give the reader historical context, e.g. religious history, philosophy, the Battle of Waterloo, slang, the King Louis-Philippe, the sewer system of Paris, and more. These passages inform the reader about the background of the people of France and give a context to the events that transpire in the novel.

Characters

Jean Valjean

(Zhahn Val-zhahn): Volume 1, Book 2, Chapter 1. Valjean is the protagonist of the story; a simple French peasant and ex-convict who tries to turn his life around but is pursued by the law. He adopts a young girl and experiences paternal love but is almost loses it at the end.

Cosette

Volume 1, Book 4, Chapter 1. Cosette is the illegitimate daughter of Felix Tholomyes, from the upper class and the working-class Fantine. She is raised as an orphan and eventually adopted by Jean Valjean. She finds happiness with Marius Pontmercy and ends up a wealthy woman.

Javert

(Zha-vert) Volume 1, Book 5, Chapter 5. Javert is a police inspector who shadows Valjean throughout the book, hoping to bring him to justice for a crime he committed just after he was released from the galleys. His life is saved by Valjean during the insurgency. He helps Valjean and Marius escape the law after the insurgency and then takes his own life.

Fantine

(Fahn-tin) Volume 1, Book 2, Chapter 2. A young working class woman in Paris she falls in love with an upper class rogue who deserts her. She returns home but to avoid the stigma of her daughter's illegitimacy she leaves her (Cosette) with a family in Montfermeil. She works at Valjean's factory in his guise as M. Madeleine. She dies before she can retrieve Cosette.

Marius Pontmercy

(POHN-mer-see) Volume 3, Book 1, Chapter 13. The son of one of Napoleon's officers and the grandson of a Royalist, Marius grows up in upper middle-class environment. He studies law and falls in love with Cosette. He joins the insurgency and almost dies but is saved by Valjean. He then marries Cosette.

M. Myriel

(Meer-ee-ell) – Volume 1, Book 1, Chapter 1 (description on p.1). The bishop is a truly good man who has little ambition other than to serve the poor and sick of his diocese. He dies early in the book, but is pivotal in guiding Valjean back on to the paths of goodness and honor.

M. Thenardier

(Ten-ard-yea) – Volume 1, Book 4, Chapter 1. A small, evil man who takes advantage of any situation he can. He turns to crime in the end but also saves the lives of Valjean and Marius in his own twisted way. His one act of heroism is to save the life of Marius's father during the Battle of Waterloo (while actually trying to rob him).

Mme. Thenardier

Volume 1, Book 4, Chapter 1. The mannish and large wife of Thenardier, she is nasty and brutal. She treats little Cosette very badly while coddling and spoiling her own daughters. She rejects her three sons and turns them onto the streets.

Eponine

(Ay-pon-in) – Volume 1, Book 4, Chapter 1. The elder of the spoiled daughters of the Thenardiers, she is not without redemption. She falls in love with Marius and is instrumental in saving Valjean and Cosette's lives. She joins the insurgency and dies in Marius's arms.

M. Gillenormand

(Jill-norm-ahn) Volume 3, Book 2, Chapter 1. The ancient and crusty but vigorous grandfather of Marius who lives a middle-class existence, somewhat fallen from his exalted position in royal circles before the Revolution. He tosses his grandson out for becoming a republican but welcomes him back and gives the young man and his bride a place to live.

Gavroche

(Gav-rosh) – Volume 3, Book 1, Chapter 13. Gavroche is the tough but appealing young adolescent son of the Thenardiers. Rejected by his parents, he lives on the streets of Paris and survives by his wits. He is charming, rude, and full of life. Gavroche dies during the insurgency.

Colonel Georges Pontmercy

Volume 3, Book 3, Chapter 2. Pontmercy is the father of Marius and the widower of M. Gillenormand's second daughter. The old man despises him and does not allow him to raise his son. Pontmercy spends most of his time gardening and contemplating. His son is only reconciled to him after Georges's death.

Enjolras

(Ehn-jol-rah) Volume 3, Book 4, Chapter 1. A blonde and handsome young man, and friend of Marius's, Enjolras is the leader of the insurgency, and a fair and honorable man. He dies during the uprising.

Fauchelevent

(Fosh-le-vehnt), Volume 1, Book 5, Chapter 6. Fauchelevent is a native of Montreuil-sur-Mer and does not like M. Madeleine (Valjean) until that man saves his life. Madeleine finds him a job as a gardener at a Paris convent and when Valjean is running for his life, Fauchelevent takes him and Cosette in, telling the nuns he is his brother.

Petit-Gervais

(Jer-vah) –Volume 1, Book 1, Chapter 13. Gervais is a little boy who Valjean comes across after leaving the bishop's residence (and stealing his silver). He takes the boy's money. Later another man is charged for this crime and Valjean takes the blame for it.

Champmathieu

(Shamp-mat-yew) – Volume 1, Book 1, Chapter 10. A simple peasant with a similar background and appearance as Valjean, he is arrested and tried for stealing money from Petit-Gervais. Valjean, now Mayor Madeleine of Montreuil-sur-Mer interrupts the trial and says *he* is the true Valjean.

M. Mabeuf

(Ma-boof) Volume 3, Book 3, Chapter 2. A good and simple man, brother of the priest who sees Georges Pontmercy visit the church to catch a glance of his son, he later tells Marius about this. They become good friends. Mabeuf later dies a heroic death during the insurgency.

Patron-Minette

Volume 3, Book 7, Chapter 3 – A gang of four men, lowest of the low, with other hangers-on. They work with Thenardier to dupe Valjean. Most of them go to jail or lose their lives.

Felix Tholomyes

(Tol –o–mees) Volume 1, Book 3, Chapter 2. Tholomyes is s young man from the upper class, a student. He keeps Fantine, a simple seamstress, who is in love with him, as is mistress. He deserts her and leaves the care of his daughter, whom he does not know, to her. He becomes a successful lawyer later in life.

Azelma

Volume 1, Book 4, Chapter 1. The second of the Thenardier daughters, her role is minor. She serves time in a woman's prison for her part in her father's villainy against Valjean. Later her father plans to take her to Panama with money he tries to extort from Marius.

Chapter Summaries

Volume 1

Book 1

Chapter 1

M. Charles-Francois Bienvenu Myriel is the Bishop of Digne and is about seventy-five years old. The year is 1815 and he has been bishop since 1806. Rumors about M. Myriel have circulated in the diocese since his arrival. His father was a councillor from Aix, so he belongs to the "nobility of the bar".

Charles Myriel's father had arranged an early marriage for him before the Revolution; during the years of the Revolution the family was dispersed and Charles went to Italy. His wife died and he had no children. Why Myriel became a priest is not known. When he returned from France from Italy he had taken holy orders.

In 1804 he was the Cure of Brignolles and went to France to request aid for his parishioners from M. le Cardinal Fesch, the uncle of the Emperor Napoleon. While Myriel was waiting to see Cardinal Fesch, Napoleon passed by and asked who was this "good man" staring at him? Later the Emperor appointed Myriel Bishop of Digne.

He arrived in Digne with his younger, devout and respectable spinster sister, Mlle Baptistine. He also brought along a bustling female servant, Madame Maglore, the same age as his sister.

Chapter 2

M. Myriel lives in the episcopal palace, a grand, large and beautiful place, about a hundred years old. There is a hospital within the grounds, a long narrow building. After his arrival he had inspected the hospital and informed the director that it was overcrowded and with inadequate outside grounds.

M. Myriel decided that part of his personal residence could be used for the care of the sick. The Bishop would live in the hospital building and the palace would become the hospital. He drew up a list of expenses to be paid from his salary – eighty percent would go to charity or religious missions. For all the years he has been at Digne M. Myriel has adhered to this budget.

M. Myriel, his sister, and their servant subsist on a small yearly stipend. The women oversee the spending of the household money and find it inadequate. M. Myriel applied to the General Council for traveling expenses; he was awarded three thousand francs. A great protest arose amongst the local burgesses and politicians. M. Myriel, with an already tight budget, levied more fees for such things as marriage banns, private baptism, etc. He continues to give generously to the poor.

M. Myriel was soon the recipient of many donations of money but he refuses to change his lifestyle and continues to help the destitute. He soon acquired the nickname of Monseigneur Bienvenu (Welcome).

Chapter 3

M. Myriel makes many visits to his parishioners in very difficult conditions. Sometimes he travels by donkey or cart and often by foot. He converted his allowance for travel expenses into alms for the poor. Wherever he goes M. Myriel praises the people of each village and parish. Like Jesus, he guides and advises by relating parables, most of his own invention.

Chapter 4

The bishop has a great sense of humor and often laughs at himself. He also sees the foolishness of others' actions but learns from them, rather than chastising them.

M. Myriel has no pride when it comes for asking for charity for the poor and shames the rich into giving. He speaks several dialects and communicates well with the poor of his diocese. The people love him. He blames the ills of society on the men who hold power. He is a great supporter of education. By his example, he sets a standard for his people to aspire to.

M. Myriel witnessed an execution of a man he had counselled. He died by guillotine and M. Myriel never entirely recovered from this experience.

Chapter 5

M. Myriel leads an austere life. He sleeps and eats little. His diocesan business keeps him very busy and most of the rest of the time he dedicates to the poor. His visitations are like a small festival for those visited. He visits the poor as long as he has the money to do so, and when it runs out, his visits the rich. Any time left over the Bishop uses to study religious writings.

Chapter 6

The building that M. Myriel lives in is very modest. There is room enough for the Bishop, his sister, their servant and the occasional guest. It is kept very clean. They keep two cows and half the milk produced goes to the patients now housed in his palace. The Bishop stays in the cow-shed during the cold weather as it is warmer there than in his bedroom. He keeps a very simple altar and when women of the diocese raise money for a new one he gives the money to the poor. Everything in the house is designed to serve the Bishop's modest needs and make do for others when the need arises. M. Myriel likes to work in the garden but in a haphazard sort of way. M. Myriel's one weakness is the set of six silver knives and forks and a soup ladle that he cannot part with. They are kept locked in a cupboard at the head of the bed, but the key is never removed. There are no locks on any of the doors of the house.

Chapter 7

Cravatte, an outlaw, had been at large in the countryside not far from the Bishop's palace and had stolen items from the Cathedral at Embrun. M. Myriel was made bishop just at the time Cravatte was terrorizing the area. He is told by the mayor that he must not venture into Cravatte's "territory" without an escort. The Bishop ignores this advice. He wants to see the shepherds who live and work in isolation and could be the victims of Cravatte and his men.
The Bishop visited with the shepherds for two weeks. He wanted some episcopal ornaments for these poor men and it wasn't long before a chest of stolen church items was returned to his humble presbytery, with a note from Cravatte.

Chapter 8

———

A senator, a Count, who had earlier protested M. Myriel's application for travel funds, has dinner with the bishop one night - they discuss philosophy. The Count is not a religious man. He believes men should strive for happiness and not worry about good and evil, but look for truth. His is a philosophy of materialism and the Bishop dismisses it as being a philosophy for the rich.

Chapter 9

The walls of the Bishop's residence have revealed some old religious paintings on the plaster, dating back centuries. This information is shared in a letter to an old friend of Myriel's sister Baptistine. The letter describes her life with the Bishop and that he is a good man. She recounts his visit to the shepherds and how the jewels of the Cathedral at Embrun were returned. Baptistine has faith that nothing bad will happen to her brother but if it does, she will die alongside of him. She also states that her brother is a royalist.

Baptistine and the servant live with the Bishop in harmony and passivity and do not question what he does. Sometimes they gently scold him for his rasher acts.

Chapter 10

There is an elderly man who lives near Digne by the name of G_____. He had been a member of the National Convention during the French Revolution, although he had not voted for the death of the king. He is considered a terrible man and an atheist, but had been allowed to remain in France. G_____ lives far from anywhere and is considered a hermit.

One day a shepherd comes to tell the Bishop that G_____ is dying. The Bishop decides to visit him. G_____ tells him he has only three hours to live. They discuss why G_____ did not vote to execute the king but he still believes the aim of the Revolution was the correct one. They discuss the deaths of innocents in all regimes.

The Bishop tells him he has come to ask his blessing, but before he can reply, G_____ dies. M. Myriel returns home and spends the night praying. The death of G_____ causes him great reflection.

Chapter 11

Despite his discussion with G_____ the Bishop is far from being a political person. M. Myriel had been made a bishop before 1809, and in July of that year the Pope was arrested and Napoleon summoned the 95 bishops to a synod. M. Myriel did not stay long, finding it had little to do with his isolated mountainous diocese. In fact, he upset some at the synod by commenting on the luxury other bishops lived in, while their parishioners were poor. M. Myriel is not a supporter of Napoleon. At heart, he is a Royalist but he recognizes that Napoleon is weakening and France is facing a crisis.

Chapter 12

The Bishop, as part of an episcopal church, has many abbes below him on the ladder. There are also "bigwigs" above him, or "big mitres". There are other bishops who are concerned with wealth, prestige, and position. Ambition can help make a bishop an archbishop and an archbishop a cardinal and may even one day aspire to be Pope. Those in their orbit can be advanced as well. Monseigneur Welcome, aka M. Myriel, does not have young priests, or abbes, about him. He is rather isolated; unlike others, he chooses to live in poverty amongst the poor. Few other bishops are like him.

Chapter 13

M. Myriel's beliefs are based on the idea of doing good works. He believes that if he follows his conscience, he is with God. He is not judgmental – he looks with the same kindness on flawed people as on the good. In a way he believes all people, himself included, are mere creatures.
Before he became a priest, the Bishop had been a less than perfect human being and had occasionally been violent. As an elderly bishop he is considered a "fine man", a good human being.
The Bishop's days are filled with good words and good deeds.
Many nights he walks in his garden, contemplating and meditating.

Chapter 14

Monseigneur Welcome's enlightenment comes from his heart and his wisdom grew out of that. He is not a deep thinker but believes in action. Many religious men try to create a personal relationship with God. Philosophers agonize over every aspect of man. This is not the Bishop's way. His path was short – it was that of the Gospel and its message is to do good works. He works amongst the miserable and is a miner of misery, seeking to extract it, without probing too deeply into the human psyche.

Book 2

Chapter 1

Early in October of 1814 a stranger travelling on foot enters Digne. He looks very wretched and those who see him are uneasy. He is a middle-aged man, his clothing is worn, and he is sweaty and weather beaten. He carries a new knapsack and a walking stick. He enters the town from a road from the south.

The man goes to the inn at the sign of the Cross of Colbas, and asks for food and lodging. The man has the necessary money. The owner secretly sends a child off with a note and when it is returned he tells the man he cannot offer him food or lodging. The man refuses to leave.

The landlord accuses him of being one Jean Valjean and shows him the note from the town-hall. Valjean leaves ignoring the people gathered, staring at him. Despairing and hungry, he looks for shelter. He enters another public house but soon a man who had stabled his horse at the other inn tells the innkeeper who the new arrival is. Even the jail will not admit him – he is told he must get himself arrested to get a room.

Valjean stops at a house – through its window he can see a family inside. He asks the man if he can stay there for payment, but the owner warns him away with a gun. Valjean wanders out into the countryside and as night falls, looks for a place to shelter him. It looks like rain and he returns to Digne and eventually meets a woman of status who after hearing he has been turned down at the inns, directs him to a place where he might find shelter.

Chapter 2

The Bishop has been working at his writing before dinner. Made ready by Madame Magloire and presided over by his sister. Madame Magloire relates the rumors about a man prowling in the neighborhood, emphasizing her dissatisfaction with local policing. She suggests they replace their ancient locks.

There is a knock on the door and the Bishop says, "Come in".

Chapter 3

Jean Valjean is at the door. The women are frightened but the Bishop stays calm. Valjean introduces himself, an ex-convict who cannot find a place to stay. He asks who they are and if he could stay, for payment. He tells him his history – nineteen years in the galleys as punishment for burglary and trying to escape from the jail. He has a yellow "passport" that shows he is an ex-convict. The Bishop offers him food and a bed and tells Valjean he is a priest (but not a bishop). In this house of Jesus Christ the hungry and suffering are welcome.

The meal begins but soon the Bishop remarks that the table is incomplete. Madame Magloire gets the rest of the silver and arranges it on the table.

Chapter 4

Later Baptistine wrote to her friend Madame Boischevron and described the conversation between her brother and Jean Valjean, after Valjean had finished his meal. He remarked that the "priest" must be very poor. He said he was heading for Pontarlier the next morning. The Bishop said he had relatives who own cheese-dairies there, hinting that it might be a refuge for Valjean.

Chapter 5

The Bishop takes Valjean to his alcove and as they pass through M. Myriel's room, Madame Magloire is putting the silverware away. Valjean has a candle in a silver candlestick and a warm goatskin has been put on his bed.

Valjean rudely asks the Bishop why he is housing him there, what if he is a killer. The Bishop replies that it is in God's hands and gives Valjean a benediction. The ex-convict is soon asleep.

Chapter 6

Jean Valjean is from a poor peasant family in Brie and was orphaned early; he had grown up illiterate. When he reached adulthood, he became a tree-pruner at Faverolles. He had one sister, a widow with seven children, and he took over the support of her family. He worked hard and went hungry. The children were often near starvation. Jean robbed a bakery to feed the children. He was sentenced to prison, partly because he was also known to practice poaching. He was sentenced to five years as a galley-slave, number 24,601. Four years on he learned his sister was in Paris, suffering greatly, and with only her youngest child.

Over the years Jean escaped several times but was always caught. Time was added to his sentence. He served nineteen years – all for stealing a loaf of bread.

Chapter 7

Valjean knows he is a man who committed a crime, that he could have got the bread by other means and that he had put his sister and her children at risk by stealing. But he also knows that a man who worked as hard as he did should not have to steal. He knows that nineteen years is too long to serve for a minor crime. He condemns society and hates it for what it does to the poor and what it has done to him. He has lost faith in religion.

Valjean is a strong, athletic man (which helped him escape), but lacks humor and is withdrawn. Nineteen years in jail has hardened him against other people. In nineteen years he has not shed a tear.

Chapter 8

The author presents an analogy: A man falls overboard and fights for his life in the sea. The ship goes on, unconcerned for his fate, as God seems to be. The man struggles for hours but eventually dies, alone, struggling against the tremendous strength of the waves. His soul goes down with his corpse.

Chapter 9

After nineteen years Jean Valjean left jail with a small amount of money earned over the years and a yellow passport that describes him as an ex-convict and a "dangerous man". The first day of freedom he found work in Grasse unloading goods but was asked for his papers; he went for his pay and received only half of his earned amount. The master made a veiled threat about prison and Jean did not protest, although he felt robbed.

Chapter 10

Jean is awakened at two a.m. by the Cathedral bell while sleeping at the Bishop's. It is his first night in a bed in twenty years. He can't get to sleep again – he has dark troubled thoughts. Eventually he gets up, takes a heavy candlestick out of his knapsack, and goes to the adjoining room where the Bishop is sleeping.

Chapter 11

The Bishop's door is not quite closed and Jean pushes it gently until it squeaks. He is sure it would rouse the household but the others slumber on. He approaches the Bishop's bed - just then the moon illuminates the good man's face which is almost radiant. Valjean, holding the heavy candlestick, is transfixed by the expression on the Bishop's face. Suddenly he goes to the cupboard where the silver in its basket is stored, takes it, and makes his escape.

Chapter 12

The next morning the Bishop finds the basket for the silver, now empty, in the garden. Madame Magloire cries out that their visitor took the silver. They can see evidence of an escape over the garden wall. The Bishop states that the silver rightly belongs to the poor, and Jean is a poor man. At breakfast the Monseigneur mentions that they do not need silver at all. They agree that it is fortunate no-one was injured during the robbery

Soon three gendarmes arrive, holding a fourth man, Valjean. They address M. Myriel as Monseigneur. Valjean is surprised as he did not know the Bishop's true status. The Bishop says that he had given Valjean the silver. He hands the candlesticks to Valjean, saying he must have forgotten them. He adds that Jean he must use them to become an honest man.

Chapter 13

Jean Valjean leaves Digne in a hurry. He does not know if she should be humiliated or touched. Out in the hills, he meets a ten year old child, singing. The child has some money and stops to play with his coins. He does not see Valjean. At one point a coin escapes and rolls toward Valjean who steps on it. The child, Little Gervais, pleads with Valjean to give him the money but the man simply raises his cudgel. The boy runs off. Later Valjean tries to find the boy but only comes across a priest, who he gives money to "for your poor". Valjean continues to look for Gervais but doesn't find him. He feels he has done something evil. He remembers the kindness of the Bishop and his last words. He weeps for the first time in nineteen years and returns to the Bishop's, kneeling in prayer at his door.

Book 3

Chapter 1

Many things had happened in the years leading up to 1817: political events, social changes, and changes in fashion – in clothing, song, and personages. History quickly forgets most of them but no details are trivial – everything is useful. In 1817 four young Parisians arranged "a fine farce".

Chapter 2

Living in Paris in 1817 are four twenty-year old students; each has his mistress: Felix Tholomyes and Fantine (the Blonde), Blacheville and Favourite; Listolier and Dahlia; and Fameuil and Zephine. The young women are from the impoverished class and other than Fantine, are experienced in life. They are friends and the young men are comrades.

The beautiful Fantine has no knowledge of her parents, has no surname; she was a child of the streets. She came to Paris at the age of fifteen. She is in love with Tholomyes, a witty young man.

Chapter 3

The four young men have planned a surprise for their mistresses. The four couples take a coach to Saint-Cloud and enjoy themselves in the suburbs of Paris. They are all beautiful. Energetic Tholomyes dominates the group. Fantine is lovely with her blonde hair and perfect teeth and her laugh. She is not conscious of her beauty and is a modest woman. There is something pure about her, something chaste.

Chapter 4

The four couples go to King's Square to see an unusual plant from India, which is attracting visitors to Saint-Cloud. From there they go to Vanvres and Issy where Tholomyes sings an old ballad to them. They cross the Seine in a boat and walk to L'Etoile. The day had been long but they are full of joy. The women were still waiting for the surprise.

Chapter 5

At dinner-time the party is at Bombarda's public house, in the Champs-Elysees. The area is thronged with people. The people of Paris are described as "frivolous and lazy" but can be roused to fight for glory.

Chapter 6
The four couples are having fun at Bombarda's. The men and women tease each other. Favourite pretends she loves Blacheville but admits to Dahlia that she does not because Blacheville is not generous and she has her eye on someone else.

Chapter 7
The group is talking and Tholomyes exhorts them to be quieter, to reflect. The others dismiss this suggestion. A bad pun is made and Tholomyes makes a mock speech about puns. He criticizes excess in anything and recommends hard work as the road to happiness and warns the men not to put their faith in women. Tholomyes admits he is drunk. He describes each of the four women. He calls Fantine a dreamer. He advises the women not to marry and advises the men to compete with each other over women, that women are "their right". Tholomyes ends his speech by exhorting them to be merry, asking Fantine to embrace him, and embracing Favourite instead.

Chapter 8
Tholomyes is ready to talk forever but is interrupted by a horse which falls in the quay. It is an old horse, exhausted from pulling a heavy load. Fantine is shocked into pity for the horse. Favourite demands their surprise. Each man kisses his mistress on her forehead and the four of them file out of the restaurant.

Chapter 9
The young women remain in the restaurant, Fantine calling to the men not to be gone long. They chat idly, watching the goings-on outside. An hour later a waiter brings a note for them. It says the men are going back to their parents, to fulfil their future roles. They ask them not to begrudge them – they have given them two years of their lives. The women laugh but later, in her room, Fantine cries for the loss of Tholomyes.

Book4

Chapter 1

In the first quarter of the 19th century there was a cook-shop in Montfermeil, near Paris. M. and Mme. Thenardier kept the shop and inn. One evening in 1818 there is a cart in front of the shop. Two pretty little girls, toddlers, are tied into a chain hanging from the cart. Their mother is pushing them, as though they are in a swing. Another woman comes along, with a three year old girl who is fast asleep. The mother, with golden hair, looks poor but is beautiful. It is Fantine. It is ten months since her young man left (the young man will become a successful lawyer); the child is his. Fantine is desperate and decided to leave Paris to return to her home town. She has only eighty francs left. The two women begin to chat – the mother of the two girls is Mme. Thenardier. Fantine tells the woman her daughter's name is Cosette although her real name is Euphrasie. The Thenardiers agree to keep Cosette while Fantine goes to the country to look for work. She pays a large part of her eighty francs in advance.

Chapter 2

The Thenardiers are of the lower middle class, a segment of society that is not known for their virtue or hard work. M. and Mme. Thenardier possess dark souls. M. Thenardier had been a soldier and the two of them have a rudimentary education. Madame is twelve or fifteen years younger than he and an avid reader of cheap romances from which she was inspired to name her daughters Eponine and Azelma.

Chapter 3

Thenardier's cook-shop and inn is not doing well. The money he received from Fantine allows M. Thenardier to pay off a pressing debt. They sold Cosette's lovely clothing - to them she is a child of charity. She wears rags and eats scraps. They write to Fantine every month, telling her the girl is doing well but they always ask for more money. M. Thenardier is vicious to Cosette and spoils her daughters who are vicious with Cosette as well. Time passes and Cosette becomes a servant of the household, even though Fantine sends more money. After three years Fantine would not have recognized Cosette. The neighbors call her "Lark" but she is a lark who never sings.

Book 5

Chapter 1

In 1818 Fantine is back is her hometown, after ten years' absence. The town, M. sur M., is prospering thanks to a successful costume jewelry business. A man named Madeleine had come to town a few years before and after saving the lives of the children of the captain of the gendarmerie, had been encouraged to set up the business.

Chapter 2

Montreuil-sur-Merhas become an important trade center. The factory made imitation jet jewelry. Father Madeleine built a large factory, with workrooms for both men and women. He employs anyone, as long as they are honest. Madeleine has built a hospital and schools for the town and helped the poor. He is a religious man. He refuses all honors offered to him but finally agrees to be mayor of M. sur M., as appointed by the King.

Chapter 3

Madeleine fulfills his duties as mayor but lives alone and rarely socializes. He likes to go for solitary walks and is a voracious reader. He often gives money away. He knows a lot about rural life. The people around him like to speculate about his past. He showed the curious his chamber contained nothing special except for two silver candlesticks. Madeleine was rumored to have a lot of money in the bank, at Lafitte's.

Chapter 4

Early in 1820 the death of Monseigneur Welcome is announced in the papers. He had become blind in his old age but had his loving and devoted sister to help him. After the Bishop's death, Mayor Madeleine appears in black, in mourning and it becomes known it is for the Bishop, although he denies being a relative. He tells people he was a servant for the family in his youth.

Chapter 5

By 1821 Mayor Madeleine is regarded as a near-saint by the people of Montreuil-sur-Mer He garners almost as much respect as the Bishop had. One person doesn't care for him – an inspector policeman named Javert, a relative newcomer to Montreuil-sur-Mer Javert had been born in prison as his father was in the galleys. To improve his status he became a policeman. He is forty years old and has no vices and few weaknesses. Javert watches Madeleine carefully.

Chapter 6

Another man who does not love Madeleine is Fauchelevent, "an ex-notary and a peasant". He is a jealous of Madeleine's success which grew while his own diminished and he became bankrupt. One day Fauchelevent falls under his cart, after his horse falls and breaks two legs. Javert has sent for a jack-screw when Madeleine arrives on the scene. The cart is sinking, crushing the man. Madeleine asks if anyone will crawl under and lift the cart but no-one volunteers. Javert says the only man who could do is one who had been a convict. Madeleine takes up the challenge and goes under the cart. He raises it just enough for Fauchelevent to escape.

Chapter 7

Madeleine takes Fauchelevent to the hospital to have him looked after and gives him a thousand francs to replace his horse and cart. He finds the man a job as a gardener at a convent in Paris. Soon after this Madeleine became mayor of Montreuil-sur-Mer Javert avoids him but when he does meet him, shows him great respect.

Chapter 8

In Montreuil-sur-MerFantine finds some happiness in working and making her own living. She hopes to be reunited with Cosette soon. Her neighbors are curious about her writing letters to the Thenardiers. She employs a letter writer who let it be known she had a child. Montreuil-sur-Merpeople are nosy and a few are malicious. She inspires jealousy in some due to her beauty. An old gossip went to Montfermeil and saw the child. Fantine is asked to leave the factory and given fifty francs.

Chapter 9

———

Although Fantine was dismissed in Mayor Madeleine's name, as he owns the factory, he knows nothing about this – he had delegated his responsibility of the woman's workroom to a trusted worker. The fifty francs was from a fund to help impoverished women.

When Fantine has paid off her debts, she is broke. She takes a low paying sewing job. She begins to pay the Thenardiers irregularly. She lives in extreme poverty and suffers poor health.

Chapter 10

Winter comes; times are harder for Fantine. Work decreases and debts increase. She needs money for Cosette so cuts off her hair and sells it. She buys a warm petticoat for Cosette but the Thenardiers gave it to their daughter Eponine. After cutting off her hair, Fantine changes; she begins to hate everyone, especially Mayor Madeleine. She takes a lover who beats and abandons her.

Fantine sells her two front teeth to a quack dentist because Cosette needs medicine. The Thenardiers demand more money. She is driven to prostitution.

Chapter 11

Fantine has entered a form of slavery, that is, prostitution. She has become a cold and dishonored figure. She is indifferent to life. Her only salvation is God.

Chapter 12

There is a leisure class of young men in Montreuil-sur-Mer– they do not work. They are not quite rich enough to be "dandies", not poor enough to be "idlers". One night Fantine, outside an officers' cafe, is insulted and accosted by one of these men, known as M. Bamatabois. She beats him with her fists and is seized by the policeman Javert. Her attacker escapes.

Chapter 13

Javert takes Fantine, terrified, to the police station. She is at Javert's mercy. In his mind as he had witnessed it, this prostitute had tried to kill a citizen. He orders Fantine to jail for six months. Fantine defends her actions, throwing herself at his mercy by saying Cosette is coming to be with her and that she cannot have her in jail. Javert is not moved, but another man has overheard Fantine begging for mercy – M. Madeleine. Fantine spits in his face but Madeleine orders Javert to let her go. Madeleine states that he will take over the care of Fantine and Cosette. She faints.

Book 6

Chapter 1

M. Madeleine has Fantine removed to the infirmary in his home.
She is very ill. When she awakes the next morning M. Madeleine is
staring at the crucifix above her bed. He enquires about her health.
M. Javert, meanwhile, has written a letter to the national department
of police, registering a complaint against Madeleine. The Mayor
writes to the Thenardiers and pays off Fantine's "debt" and tells
them to bring Cosette to Montreuil-sur-Mer Thenardier sees another
chance to exploit Cosette. He draws up a large bill for her care.
Madeleine pays, and demands they send the child. The Thenardiers
do not and meanwhile, Fantine's health worsens.

Chapter 2

One day Javert comes to speak to Madeleine about the incident
concerning Fantine six weeks previously. Javert's manner is cold
but respectful. He tells Madeleine he wants the mayor to dismiss
him. To hand in his resignation is not enough, he must be punished.
He admits he told the authorities that Madeleine is an ex-convict –
Jean Valjean. He then says the real Valjean has been found: a man
by the name of Champmathieu – the facts of his life fit those of
Valjean. Javert has even seen him and is sure it is Valjean.
Madeleine dismisses Javert but does not allow him to resign.

Book 7

Chapter 1

Madeleine visits Fantine, taking Sister Simplice with him, a nun who works in the infirmary. The sister is a gentle woman but a woman of truth. Madeleine and Sister Simplice become fixtures in Fantine's life, visiting her in her room. Madeleine promises that Cosette will be sent for soon. Fantine has little time left.

Chapter 2

M. Madeleine goes to Master Scaufflaire, who rents out horses and cabriolets. He asks M. Scaufflaire for a good horse that can cover forty leagues in two days with a carriage. He does not say where he is going. He goes home to await his journey the next day.

Chapter 3

Madeleine is indeed Jean Valjean. After meeting Little Gervais he became a changed man. He sold the Bishop's silver, kept the candlesticks, and settled in Montreuil-sur-Merand did good things for the town. He wants to conceal his real name and serve God. Javert has left him in a confused state. Guilt about Gervais has been rekindled and he fears Champmathieu is paying for his misdeeds. Then he feels some relief – he is safe, and perhaps Javert will leave town. After much thought he throws all of his objects from his life as Jean Valjean, including the candlesticks, into the fire but rescues them in the end. He still does not know what to do.

Chapter 4

Madeleine paces for hours, finally falling asleep only to dream. It is a dream of wandering and confusion. He wakes up and in a haze realizes the carriage he ordered has arrived.

Chapter 5

Madeleine gets in the little carriage, a tilbury, and seems unsure where of where to go even after a long night of thinking and confusing dreams. He begins to head to Arras. On his way out of town he collides with a cabriolet but does not notice until he reaches Hesdin where the stableman points out damage. He may have to stay overnight while it is fixed. Then an old woman offers a cabriolet he can hire. He sets out again and comes upon many obstacles on his journey as he heads to Arras.

Chapter 6

Fantine is very ill; she is only twenty-five but looks like an old woman. M. Madeleine usually comes at three but today does not which upsets her. She begins to sing song she used to sing to Cosette and becomes convinced Madeleine has gone to get her. The doctor comes and finds his patient is doing well.

Chapter 7

It takes Madeleine fourteen hours to reach Arras, normally done in six. He makes arrangements to return to Montreuil-sur-Meron the mail wagon. He finds the courthouse; Champmathieu's trial is in progress. Madeleine uses his position as a mayor to obtain a seat in the crowded court.

Chapter 8

Madeleine is known far and wide and his good reputation has reached Arras so he is asked to sit behind Monsieur le President. He vacillates but in the end decides that he will sit in on the trial.

Chapter 9

The courtroom is full of people, officials and spectators. No-one pays attention to Madeleine. He seeks out the man on trial who is identified as Jean Valjean by the prosecution. The defendant calls himself Champmathieu and he is very rough looking. One of the men on the jury is Bamatabois, the man who had accosted Fantine. Champmathieu is accused of stealing apples and he is a man with a record, an ex-convict, and has been at large for years after committing highway robbery on a child called Little Gervais. The prosecutor presents a strong case against the accused.

Chapter 10

The accused, a wheelwright, recounts his difficult life. He denies stealing the apples, windfalls, and says he is not Valjean. A statement by Inspector Javert is read; Javert knows the man as Jean Valjean. Three convicts are brought in who identify him as Valjean. M. Madeleine calls to the three men, all known to him, from his seat behind the President.

Chapter 11
Before he could be stopped, Madeleine walks towards the three witnesses. They say they do not know him. Madeleine turns to the jury and tells them to release the prisoner because *he* is Jean Valjean. The district-attorney calls for a doctor; he fears Madeleine is insane. Madeleine says the money he stole from Little Gervais is in the ashes of his fireplace. He mentions facts about the witnesses that only a close friend could know. He leaves the court, inviting the district-attorney to arrest him. The jury frees Champmathieu.

———

Book 8

Chapter 1

Madeleine returns to Montreuil-sur-Merhoping to see Fantine. Sister Simplice tells him Fantine thought he had gone to get Cosette. The Sister notices that Madeleine's hair has gone white. Sister tells him Fantine won't know he has returned and he can go to Paris and fetch Cosette. Madeleine looks in on her; she is asleep.

Chapter 2

The doctor arrives and tells Fantine her child is there. She is overjoyed. He says he will bring Cosette in when she is better. She turns and asks Madeleine many questions about the girl. She happily plans their future together. Suddenly Fantine stops speaking – Javert has entered the room.

Chapter 3

Champmathieu has been freed and the district-attorney has his sights set on Madeleine. An order is issued for his arrest, sent to Javert in Montreuil-sur-Mer The inspector happily proceeds to Madeleine's.

Chapter 4

Fantine, seeing Javert, implores Madeleine (now known as Valjean) to save her. She thinks Javert has come for her. Javert grabs Valjean by the collar and she screams. Valjean begs Javert to allow him time to get Cosette. Fantine raises herself and quickly falls back, dead. Valjean rips off the metal headboard and threatens Javert with it – then says his goodbyes to Fantine. He gives himself up to Javert.

Chapter 5

The arrest of the mayor causes a commotion in Montreuil-sur-Mer His past history is made known. His portress waits for him later, expecting him at his usual time. Eventually Valjean arrives; he has escaped from jail. He retrieves the candlesticks the Bishop had given him and leaves the money he stole from Little Gervais. Soon he hears Javert asks Sister Simplice if she has seen Valjean. She lies and says no and Javert leaves. Valjean is able to escape.

Volume 2

Book 1

Chapter 1

In 1861, a year before the narrator is telling this story, a traveller is walking in Belgium, from Nivelles, heading to La Hulpe. He passes several settlements and comes to a door in the style of Louis XIV with an old rusty knocker. A peasant woman came out. She tells him he is at Hougomont – he looks over the hedges and sees the battlefield of Waterloo.

Chapter 2

The traveller goes through the door at Hougomont and passes into the courtyard where the English had held out for seven hours against Napoleon's armies. In the chapel a massacre took place. The well is full of the skeletons of the three hundred dead, and perhaps some not dead, thrown in. The garden is in ruins. Six hundred men died there in a mere minutes. In the orchard fifteen hundred men died in less than an hour. Napoleon's forces met their Waterloo in the field beyond.

Chapter 3

The narrator returns to June 18th, 1815 to the day of the battle. It had rained at Waterloo and this fact changed the fate of Europe. The artillery could not manoeuvre until the ground dried; Napoleon was a man who relied on the artillery. He had a brilliant battle plan but he was destined to lose this important battle.

Chapter 4

The narrator explains the Battle of Waterloo by using asking the reader to imagine the letter "A" as the layout of the battle. The British are at the top of the "A", led by Wellington, and the French are at the bottom, led by Napoleon Bonaparte.

Chapter 5

The first part of the Battle of Waterloo was more troubling for the English than the French. Napoleon attacked the center of the "A" and then feinted left to Hougomont. This did not draw Wellington there as hoped and the battle raged. What exactly happened moment to moment is not known. In the afternoon a crucial point was reached.

Chapter 6

By late afternoon a British general, Picton, is dead. Other leaders would die that day. Hougomont was still controlled by the French. Thousands of soldiers are dead; half of their horses are dead as well. The British hope to take the center, snatching victory from defeat. The afternoon does not go well for them and Napoleon victoriously predicts a retreat.

Chapter 7

The Emperor Napoleon was in high spirits that afternoon. The previous night Napoleon had been convinced victory would be his and thousands of British soldiers and their allies would be taken prisoner.

Chapter 8

The battle progressed through the day, with gains and losses on both sides. Napoleon, felt invincible. Wellington began to retreat into the forest of Soignes and the Emperor sent a messenger to Paris to announce a victory.

Chapter 9

Napoleon had a formidable squadron of over three thousand men on huge horses. They attacked the retreated English infantry, which numbered about the same. The French came upon a ravine and a third of the horses fell in. The turning point of the battle began then. The author blames the loss on God's will; he had determined that Napoleon would lose.

Chapter 10

The English infantry and their allies, divided into battalions faced what was left of Napoleon's squadron. The conflict lasted two hours. The casualties are high, from the lowest soldier to the highest ranks.

Chapter 11

After a number of events that changed the course of the battle, the British and their allies, led by the Prussians, were able to bombard the reserves behind Napoleon.

Chapter 12

The French were driven back. In late afternoon and the clouds parted for the first time that day. The French Marshal, Ney, tried to get himself killed by the English but failed.

Chapter 13

The French began to surrender. Napoleon told his men not to give up. The retreat left many dead, as men fled and were crushed to death. Napoleon was taken by the allies, by two soldiers named Bernard and Bertrand, as he dismounted from his horse.

Chapter 14

Many more men die after the Battle is over. There were more corpses than survivors.

Chapter 15

Among the French, there was a hero, an obscure officer named Cambronne. He was the winner at Waterloo, not Wellington. He survived the battle and responded "*merde!*" when told by the English to surrender.

Chapter 16

Waterloo was a battle of confusion but its importance has changed the truth of its history. The part men played means nothing, in the author's eyes. The victory is due to God. "Waterloo is a battle of the first order, won by a captain of the second" (Wellington); it was won by English resolution and English blood – won by her army, not her leader. Wellington the man was not a hero; it is the country itself which is heroic.

Chapter 17

Napoleon had overthrown the old order after the Revolution and with his defeat the monarchy is restored, with Louis XVIII.

Chapter 18

Napoleon's defeat at Waterloo means the end of his dictatorship. The Empire of France falls into gloom. A new France is in the making, one that supports Liberty. Napoleon fallen is more venerated than Napoleon undefeated.

Chapter 19

After the last cannon-shot at Waterloo, the plain at Mont-Saint-Jean remained deserted. The English are encamped where the French had been. The village of Hougomont has been burned. The rear-guard, not having seen action, arrived. The dead are robbed, despite Wellington's orders that robbers would be shot. A prowler moved amongst the dead, and found a French officer, and took his jewelry and his money. The officer regains consciousness and asks the man his name – it is Thenardier. The officer introduces himself as Pontmercy.

Book 2

Chapter 1

It is 1823 and the newspapers have told the story of M. Madeleine –
his history in Montreuil-sur-Merand his true identity – Jean Valjean,
a convict who had been jailed for theft in 1796. Valjean had
removed half a million francs from the local bank and had secured it
in a place unknown. Another article names a woman of the town as
his "concubine" who died from shock when he was arrested.
Valjean stood trial for robbing a young boy eight years previously –
Little Gervais. He was condemned to death and taken to the prison
at Toulon. His businesses in Montreuil-sur-Merare shut and the
town's prosperity dies.

Chapter 2

At Montfermeil, the home of the Thenardiers, there is a superstition.
The devil uses their forest to hide his treasures. A black man with
horns has been seen digging holes there. It is only a myth, but the
myth persists.
There is an old road-laborer named Boulatrouelle in the area who is
regarded as "peculiar". He is often in the woods, digging so the
locals link him with the devil. In time they lose interest in
Boulatrouelle – other than the school-master and Thenardier, who
knows Boulatrouelle is an ex-convict. They get him drunk and he
says he has seen a man he knows, but will not name, bury a coffer
than must contain money. He has dug and dug but cannot locate the
coffer.

Chapter 3

Late in 1823 the ship *Orion* arrives in the port of Toulon. It is the
Restoration in France and the country has been fighting the Spanish.
Militarily France does not do well and this enrages the democratic
spirit that has become stronger in the country. The *Orion* puts into
port as it needs repairs. It is a simple wooden sailing vessel. It has
sprung a leak. While being repaired a topman loses his balance and
grabs a rope, hanging perilously over the shipyard. A convict climbs
up to save him and is successful, but then he falls into the sea. It is
Jean Valjean.

Book 3

Chapter 1

In 1823 Montfermeil was just simple village in the forest. It is a difficult place to supply with water. Thenardier paid someone to get the water he needs each day for their inn. Cosette had remained with the Thenardiers after the death of her mother. No more money is forthcoming. She now fetches the water for no payment.
A small fair comes to Montfermeil around Christmas time. Cosette is in the inn's pub, dressed in rags, sitting under a table, knitting stockings for the Thenardier children. There is now a three year old son, unloved by his parents.

Chapter 2

Thenardier has just turned fifty, Mme Thenardier is almost forty. The latter does much of the housework around the inn. She is a large manly woman with a large voice. Cosette is her only servant. Thenardier is a small healthy man, although he appears weak. He is always looking for ways of improving his situation, even at the expense of others. He exaggerates his military career at Waterloo, where he was in the rear-guard. After the war, he set up his inn in Montfermeil, partly with what he had stolen off the corpses at Waterloo. He is in serious debt.
Thenardier hates everyone and blames others for his misfortunes. His wife is under his control. She fears only him, and loves only her daughters. In their own way, they both abuse Cosette, who is now eight.

Chapter 3

New travellers have arrived and Cosette must get fetch water in the dark, which terrifies her. Madame Thenardier orders Cosette to get water and to buy a loaf of bread.

Chapter 4

The country fair is still on, with many booths illuminated. Opposite the inn is a toy-shop. A large doll, almost two feet high, is coveted by all the girls – and too expensive for the people of Montfermeil. Cosette looks at the doll as she leaves the inn, thinking what a wonderful thing it is. Thenardier yells at her to get the water.

Chapter 5

Cosette heads to the spring in the forest to fetch the water. She soon passes the outskirts of the town and is in the fields outside the village. She stares into the deep woods and is overcome by fear. She knows if she doesn't get the water the Thenardiers will punish her. At the spring she unknowingly loses the money for bread in the water. Terrified of the darkness Cosette slowly makes her way back with the heavy pail. Suddenly a man appears out of nowhere and helps her with the pail.

Chapter 6

On that Christmas Day in 1823 there is a man wandering about Paris. His is poorly dressed, in a yellow coat, but clean. He looks to be over sixty years old, but with the vigor of a man of fifty. The King, Louis XVIII, followed a certain route around Paris each day, passing by the Boulevard de l'Hopital where the man wandered. The king's companion noticed him and his guard tried to follow him. The man finds a coach going to Lagny (near Montfermeil) and climbs aboard. The coachman puts it about that there is an untrustworthy stranger in town. The man heads to Montfermeil, through the fields, and this is the man who Cosette meets.

Chapter 7

Cosette is not frightened of the man in the yellow coat. She asks her a few questions, including if she has a mother. She does not know. He asks her name and he realizes she is Fantine's daughter. She tells him Mme Thenardier has sent her for water. When they reach the tavern door, Cosette takes the bucket so Madame will not beat her.

Chapter 8

Cosette looks at the doll before they go inside. She tells Madame that the man is looking for a room. They think he is a beggar but he says he will pay their rate for any room. They double their rate and a customer calls them on this but Thenardier says he always charges poor people double, to discourage them. Cosette goes back under the table to knit and the man observes how poorly she looks. Madame Thenardier asks about the bread; Cosette lies and says the baker was closed. When she asks for the money back the girl realizes it is gone. The stranger comes to her rescue and gives Thenardier a coin of larger value saying he found it on the floor. The traveller pays the Thenardiers so that Cosette can have a short time to play. Cosette takes the Thenardier girls' doll to play with. When Madame discovers this she yells at Cosette and the girl begins to cry. Meanwhile the man in the yellow coat leaves. He returns with the fabulous doll from the toy-stall and give it to Cosette. The Thenardiers are astounded and Cosette is overwhelmed. She begins to play and eventually goes to bed, taking her doll. The man stays up until three in the morning, when at last he goes to bed, led by M. Thenardier to the best chamber.

The man in the yellow coat goes looking for Cosette who is sleeping in a rat's nest of old papers, straw, and dust – with a ragged straw pallet and coverlet. She sleeps in her clothes. Although it is Christmas Eve, nothing has been left in her shoes, unlike Eponine and Azelma who have money left in theirs by the good fairy. The man in the yellow coat places a Louis d'or in Cosette's battered shoe.

Chapter 9

Thenardier makes up a bill for the man in the yellow coat – overcharging him. His wife tells the stranger things are hard for them, due to their expenses for Cosette or "Lark" as she is called. He offers to take her off their hands. Madame is willing but Thenardier wants to talk with the man first. He asks to see his passport, his identification. Thenardier tells the man he needs fifteen hundred francs to pay a debt. Soon Madame fetches Cosette who leaves with the man, carrying her doll and wearing new clothing.

Chapter 10

Madame Thenardier intimates that her husband should have asked for more from the stranger – he sets off and catches up with them. He offers his money back for the return of the girl. The other man pulls out the note written by Fantine just before her death, instructing him to collect Cosette. Thenardier demands even more money; the man picks up his large cudgel. They go on their way and Thenardier follows but soon gives up.

Chapter 11

Jean Valjean escaped from the *Orion* – he had money but no clothing and nowhere to go, although he found some places to stay where he was safe. He reached Paris and then headed to Montfermeil to find Cosette. They head to Paris. Cosette is weary, and he carries her on his back, with her doll Catherine.

Book 4

Chapter 1

The deserted Gorbeau hovel is in the Boulevard de l'Hopital in remote area of Paris. It is a humble building where a lawyer had once lived.

Chapter 2

Jean Valjean takes Cosette to the Gorbeau house. He has the keys. Upstairs there is a modestly furnished room with a dressing-room. The latter has a folding bed and he lays Cosette there. Valjean had prepared the house the night before. Cosette sleeps peacefully through the night and when she wakes up Valjean tells her to play.

Chapter 3

Jean Valjean, now fifty-five, has never loved anything. He hardly remembers his sister and her children. Cosette has moved his heart in a fatherly way. Cosette too, has never loved and has only experienced rejection. Now, searching for a father, her heart reaches out to Valjean.

One other person lives in the house – an old woman who does the housekeeping and takes his rent, which he has paid six months in advance.

Chapter 4

Valjean and Cosette live a quiet life; they go out for walks in deserted areas. Those who see them think he is a poor man. But he is also known as one who gives to the poor himself. The old housekeeper is an inquisitive woman. She spies on Valjean and discovers he has money which he later asks her to exchange. She gossips about this to others and snoops through his coat.

Chapter 5

There is a praying beggar at the nearby church of Saint-Menard; sometimes Valjean gives him money. The man is a former policeman. One evening Valjean thinks he recognizes him – he looks like Javert. A few nights later he hears footsteps on the stairs and again at daybreak. He looks through the keyhole and sees Javert.

Later the housekeeper tells him there is a new lodger, Dumont. Later, in the dark, he takes Cosette and they go out.

Book 5

Chapter 1

Valjean takes a circuitous route away from the house, making sure that he is not being followed. The moonlight helps. Cosette does not question what they are doing. Valjean puts his faith in God to guide them. After awhile he realizes three men are following them. A fourth man joins them and Valjean sees from a hidden doorway that one of them is Javert.

Chapter 2

Valjean manages to get away, carrying Cosette. They reach the quay, and the Austerlitz Bridge where he pays two tolls. They cross in the shadow of a cart. On the other side he sees the shadows of four men just beginning to cross. He enters rue du Chemin-Vert-Saint-Antoine, hoping to escape the men's notice.

Chapter 3

Valjean takes a road that leads to open country. He carries Cosette to maintain a good pace. At one point he perceives that someone has been posted at a spot with the purpose of stopping him. He feels trapped.

Chapter 4

Valjean and Cosette are in the Droit-Mur lane. There is a strange and gloomy building on one side, securely locked. There are drain pipes coming out of the house into the street but they are in poor shape, no good for climbing. He can see no way to reach the top of a three story house.

Chapter 5

Suddenly seven or eight soldiers with bayonets arrive in the next street, rue Polonceau. He can see two of Javert's men among them. He will have to scale the wall - but Cosette poses a problem. Valjean remembers ropes are stored in boxes at various points for the use of lamp lighters. He ties Cosette to a rope using his cravat, takes the rope in his teeth, and climbs the wall. He reaches the top and then pulls Cosette up just as the pursuing men arrive. Valjean slides down the roof to the other side, where it is near the ground, and jumps to safety with Cosette.

———

Chapter 6

They find themselves in a large grassy garden with many trees, bushes, a melon patch and a well. There are piles of firewood and a statue with a damaged face. The building's windows are grated and there are no lights. Valjean puts his shoes on again and Cosette trembles with fright. They can hear the distant voices of their pursuers. Suddenly they hear a hymn being sung from the house.

Chapter 7

It is after midnight. Cosette, leaning against Valjean, is very cold. To keep her quiet, Valjean had told her Madame Thenardier was after her. She is still afraid; he tells her Madame is gone to her relief. He looks into the windows of the building and sees a figure lying on the ground as though in prayer. The figure has a rope around its neck. Valjean flees in terror and returns to the sleeping Cosette.

Chapter 8

Valjean hears the faint sound of a bell. He sees a man in the melon beds and fears it is one of Javert's men. He hides Cosette in a shed and watches the man; a bell rings whenever he moves.
Cosette is very cold and is near unconsciousness; Valjean fears she is dead or dying. She needs warmth.

Chapter 9

Valjean approaches the man in the garden, ready with money to ask a favor. The man recognizes him, calling him "Father Madeleine", and is overjoyed to see him. Finally Valjean recognizes Fauchelevent, who reminds him that he saved his life. This is the Petit-Picpus convent where Valjean found him a job as a gardener. Fauchelevent agrees to do whatever he can for Valjean who swears him to secrecy.

Chapter 10

The police always search Paris for a person on the run. Javert was not sad to read in the newspaper that Valjean was dead. Later he heard about the abduction of a girl from Montfermeil and the circumstances made him think of Valjean; he wonders if he was the perpetrator. Javert went to Montfermeil to find out more and was convinced that it was not Valjean. Later he heard about the man from Montfermeil who lived in the parish of Saint-Medard with a girl and gave the poor alms. Javert is successful in tracking him down and then the chase is on. He believes he has Valjean trapped but now he has lost him again. He orders his men to keep looking for Valjean.

Book 6

Chapter 1

To get into the convent, one had to pass the porter. A narrow staircase reaches the next floor – and in one of the rooms is a grated hole. A password must be said to enter the room. Behind another grated window there is a voice that belongs to a Bernardine nun. This is their convent.

Chapter 2

The nuns are the subjects of Saint Benoit, of the Benedictine monks. They spend much time fasting and praying (sometimes with a rope around their neck, as Valjean had seen). They avoid even looking at men. Some of them go mad.

Chapter 3

A girls' school is attached to the convent, mostly for girls of wealthy and noble Catholic families. The girls conform to the practices of the convent.

Chapter 4

At a certain time each day the girls are allowed into the garden to play. They tell stories and jokes and riddles. The children have nicknames for some of the nuns and for different parts of the convent.

Chapter 5

The refectory, or dining room, opens up into the garden. The food is plain and it is eaten in silence. While they eat the children listen to readings about the lives of the saints. If they break the silence, they must lick the ground. They are still normal girls. They are obsessed about finding the young man in the neighborhood who plays the flute three times a day – and finally find out he is old and penniless.

Chapter 6

There are three buildings belonging to the convent – the Great Convent, the school, and the Little Convent, for aged nuns of all orders. Some are society women who have left society. A church stands between the Great Convent and the school.

Chapter 7

Some of the girls belong to the convent's choir. The children are treated better than the nuns treat themselves but the rule of silence still prevails. Much communication is done with bells and the children know what bell and which peals represent.

Chapter 8

The convent is situated in an old part of Paris and the streets around it are more ancient than the city itself. The buildings of the convent take up a large trapezium shaped piece of land.

Chapter 9

One of the residents of the Little Convent is a one hundred year old woman who moved in society knowing men in high places. She tells many stories and amuses the girls. She will not receive visitors in the gloomy parlor.

Chapter 10

There is another Benedictine order, the nuns of the Holy Sacrament, but they are distinct from the Bernardines of the Petit-Picpus.

Chapter 11

After the Revolution the convent of the Petit-Picpus was in decline. The numbers of nuns dropped. It will not be long before the Little Convent and the school disappear.

Book 7

Chapter 1

The convent is similar to all the places of worship and dedication that are found in all religions, even those from pagan times.

Chapter 2

Monasticism is the mark of a society that has not evolved. The prosperity of monasteries means that the poor suffer. By the nineteenth century claustration has had its day. The cloisters are filled with death, not life.

Chapter 3

Monasticism depopulates. Claustration causes castration, in a figurative sense. Hand-in-hand with feudalism, it was the scourge of Europe. It is an antiquated institution that managed to survive into the nineteenth century but it is in decline.

Chapter 4

Men have the right to live in communities and also the right to live in their own dwellings, to shut out the world, to move as they please. The ideal is equality, no one person with more power than another. A monastery is like a republic. But they also do something else.

Chapter 5

In monasteries, men pray as do women in convents. They pray to God, an infinity which raises many questions. Does it think? Does it love? Democracy upholds the right of man to worship but not to give power to religious institutions.

Chapter 6

Prayer is good, as long as it is sincere. Some may discount the infinite, or God, and there are those who deny the sun – the blind. Man lives by his belief in the infinite even more than he lives on bread. Man has two "motors" driving him – faith and love.

Chapter 7

Monasticism wants to withdraw from the world in order to find the truth – but the truth of God comes from living within the world. A convent or a monastery is a contradiction – one suffers to enjoy. One gives up this world for the next – but it was God's plan for man to live in *this* world.

Chapter 8

Faith is necessary for man. We must remember the dead and contemplate death. Thought and prayer must be balanced. Existence in the convent is one that is one of being halfway between life and death. The nuns are to be both pitied and envied, for their error and for their devotion.

Book 8

Chapter 1

Valjean arrives at this convent with Cosette. In a way they have "fallen from the sky", from the convent roof. A bed is made for Cosette in a small out building. Valjean rests on a pile of straw but does not sleep. He is determined to remain at the convent. Fauchelevent cannot figure out how Valjean got there, especially with the child. He has not heard any news from Montreuil-sur-Mer He thinks Valjean's flight may be due to financial problems. He is determined to help the man who saved his life. He is a peasant but an intelligent one.

Fauchelevent tells Valjean that he cannot leave the hut. The nuns are currently distracted by the death of one of their own. The gardener is worried about the students finding Valjean and Cosette. He tries to think of a plan to bring Valjean and Cosette into the convent with the consent of the nuns.

As gardener, he must nail all coffins shut. He goes to see the prioress about this task.

Chapter 2

The prioress, normally cheerful, is agitated. Fauchelevent, who the nuns call Father Fauvent, tells her he has a request to make. Fauchelevent has always paid close attention to what goes on in the convent, for example, he knows what the different peals of bells mean. He goes into a long story about his life and his time at the convent and concludes by saying he has a brother who is no longer young that he wants to come to live with him. He adds that the brother has a small daughter.

Chapter 3

82

The prioress leaves Fauchelevent alone for a quarter of an hour. When she returns she explains she needs two men and a lever to lift a stone to open a vault. The dead nun, Mother Crucifixion, must be placed in the vault under the altar but not in her coffin. Fauchelevent protests that no-one can be buried under an altar. She says it was her wish, and the wishes of the dead must be honored. Fauchelevent will nail the coffin shut but the nun's body will not be in it; it will be filled with dirt. The nun's corpse will be placed in the vault without anyone's knowledge. The prioress agrees that his "brother" can come to the convent to assist him.

Chapter 4

Fauchelevent returns to the cottage where Valjean and Cosette are. He tells them he has permission to bring them there but first he must get them out so they can return the next morning. He explains the problem of the coffin – he does not think putting dirt in will work – the pallbearers will know it is not a body. Valjean says he will get in the coffin, that it is a way for him to be taken out of the convent. He will escape from the coffin at the graveyard. Fauchelevent says he can handle the gravedigger, drunk (his usual state) or sober. The plan is set.

Chapter 5

The next day a hearse heads to the Vaugirard cemetery. Fauchelevent brings up the rear of the procession. The cemetery is falling into disuse. The nun has been buried in the vault and Jean Valjean is inside the coffin, ready for "burial". Fauchelevent is happy with how things are going. He has the gravedigger, Mestienne, under his control, so is not concerned about him. However, when they reach the cemetery, there is a new gravedigger – Mestienne is dead. This gravedigger cannot be enticed with drink.

Chapter 6

Valjean experiences dizziness when the coffin is lowered by rope into the grave. He hears the burial service and is aware of shovelfuls of earth being thrown onto the coffin. He passes out.

Chapter 7

When the hearse, priest, and choir boy had left, Fauchelevent declared that he would pay for the wine, but still the gravedigger would not agree to drink with him. Finally the man agrees, but only to drink after the grave is filled. As the gravedigger bends over Fauchelevent picks his pocket – taking the card he needs to get in and out of the cemetery, the latter before sundown. Fauchelevent asks him if he has it and points out if he doesn't, there will be a fine to pay if he isn't out before sundown. He tells him to go and he will bury the corpse. When the man leaves Fauchelevent pulls open the coffin. Valjean looks dead but soon revives. They fill in the grave and then go to the gravedigger's modest house (he has a wife and seven children) – they return his pick and shovel and his card.

Chapter 8

Cosette had been left at the fruiterer's. She is very upset and is overjoyed to see Valjean. Fauchelevent takes them to see the prioress. He introduces Valjean as Ultime Fauchelevent. Valjean introduces Cosette as his granddaughter. Valjean is given a bell to tie around his knee to warn the females a man is nearby. The prioress thinks Cosette might make a good nun and takes her on as a charity pupil.

Chapter 9

Cosette now wears the uniform of the school. Valjean keeps the little outfit of clothes he had bought for her. Fauchelevent is happier because he has to work less and because Valjean, who he thinks of as M. Madeleine, buys him snuff. The nuns never notice that the "other Fauvent" never leaves the grounds; the elder Fauvent always runs the errands. It is just as well, as Javert has watched the convent for weeks. Valjean is happy to work as a gardener again and spends an hour a day with Cosette. Both are content. The years pass and she grows up.

Volume 3

Book 1

Chapter 1

Paris has many homeless and poverty stricken children, ragged and hungry. However knowing they are, they are children, they are innocents. Each child is "the little one" of Paris. One of their names is "gamin".

Chapter 2

Not all the children of Paris's streets are destitute – some have a home, but prefer the freedom of the street. Some make money by doing little jobs for the wealthy or *bourgeoisie*. The child has his own wildlife – the insects and vermin of Paris. And the street urchins have their own humor.

Chapter 3

The gamins usually have enough *sous* to go to the theatre in the evening, where they huddle together in the cheapest seats. They are not literary sophisticates but it does not stop them from making scathing and ribald comments on the performances.

Chapter 4

The street urchins, the gamins, eventually grow up. They have learned their lessons on the streets. The events of their lives are purely the result of luck – good or bad.

Chapter 5

The gamin loves the city but he also loves time to himself. There is an air of melancholy about the poor, despite their seemingly high spirits. The city has an air of melancholia. The poor children are found everywhere, in the core and in the suburbs. The gangs of children are mostly boys but there are girls too.

Chapter 6

The police force grew in the latter part of the nineteenth century; before this Paris had many "stray" children, some were actually homeless. At the age of fifteen, boys could be commandeered as galley slaves.

Chapter 7

Executions, by the guillotine, are a staple of the gamin's entertainment. He finds them amusing – he can climb any structure to get a better view. Those that are led to execution become their heroes, the stuff of pop culture. What they are wearing and fascinates the gamins.

Chapter 8

At night the gamins often jump into the Seine River. They will go into the sewers to avoid the police, who keep close track of Paris's gamin population. The gamins of all eras quickly learn what they need to know, just to survive. Most of them have little respect for the clergy but they often know the names of policemen, and a lot about the character of each one.

Chapter 9

Some gamins later become successful. They have spirit, even when their health may be very poor. They live; they endure, even when they are unhappy.

Chapter 10

The only way to improve the gamin's life is through education, in its purest form – through enlightenment; in a figural sense, letting in the light, which promotes life. Anything that can be found elsewhere can be found in Paris, in the present, and in the past. In a figurative sense, Paris is every classical city that had existed before.

Chapter 11

Paris is a city that can laugh at itself with its joviality and its gaiety. It can also explode. It knows how to celebrate and how to commemorate. When Paris "is not scolding, it is laughing". It is daring, willing to take a chance.

Chapter 12

The true face of Paris is seen in the faces of its poor, of its gamins. The author exhorts the philosophers, the idealists, the intellectuals, to make use of what the poor can offer – they must be enlightened so that their pure souls can be improved with noble ideals.

Chapter 13

Eight or nine years after Jean Valjean and Cosette began to live at the convent, a gamin lives on Boulevard du Temple. He is eleven or twelve years old, a laughing boy with an empty heart, neglected by his parents. He had been kicked out of his home. He is only merry because he is free. His family lives in the Gorbeau hovel where Valjean had lived years before. His parents have two daughters, whom his mother loves; she does not love him. The boy's name is Gavroche and his family name is Jondrette. Next door to his parents lives a poor young man named M. Marius.

Book 2

Chapter 1

In the 1860's, in the Paris neighborhood of Mardis, a man named Luc-Esprit Gillenormand is remembered, although many who knew him were old. In 1831 he is still alive, vigorous and over ninety. He is from a bygone era – a member of the "haughty" bourgeoisie of the eighteenth century.

Chapter 2

Gillenormand owns a house in the Marais, and lives in an apartment on the first floor. He has had two wives. He can be charming when he wants to be. With his wives he was sullen but charming with his mistresses. He is a connoisseur of art and dresses in the fashions of his youth. Gillenormand has never approved of the French Revolution.

Chapter 3

At sixteen Gillenormand had been in love with a dancer his own age. He was sought after by older women. In his youth, he had had no use for politics. He could be very coarse, and vulgar around women. His godfather predicted he would be a genius.

Chapter 4

Gillenormand is very proud of receiving school prizes from the Duc de Nivernais. He loved the Bourbons and told everyone how he had managed not to be executed during the Reign of Terror. Gillenormand hopes to live a hundred years.

Chapter 5

Gillenormand has a philosophy for an unhappily married man – let his wife control   the purse-strings and she will not interfere with other business even if she ruins him financially. This is what happened to him– his second wife left him with just enough to live on. He has a male servant he calls Basque and a female he calls Nicolette.

Chapter 6

One day a baby boy is brought, supposedly his own son by a servant-maid. Gillenormand was eighty-four at the time and denies paternity but agrees the child will be taken care of. The next year another baby boy arrived, and this time he sent both back to their mother, Magnon. He pays maintenance and visits occasionally. Gillenormand has one surviving daughter, an unmarried woman in her fifties.

Chapter 7

Gillenormand still has his hair, now gray, and dresses well. He receives guests only in the evening, after dining at five. He considers daytime to be "vulgar".

Chapter 8

M. Gillenormand had another daughter, who had died around the age of thirty – she would be in her forties now. The two girls had different but both had wings – the elder was a goose, the younger an angel. The younger died, after marrying the man of her dreams. The surviving daughter is very prudish, both a vice and a virtue. She is also bigoted and religious. Mlle Gillenormand keeps house for her father. With them lived his grandson.

Book 3

Chapter 1

M. Gillenormand was accepted in society for he was witty and charming. In 1817 he was part of a salon of Royalists hosted by an impoverished Baroness, known as Baronne de T. He attended the salon with his daughter and his grandson, who was then seven years old. The boy was the son of Gillenormand's son-in-law, who was regarded as a disgrace.

Chapter 2

In 1817 in the town of Vernon there lived a married man of about fifty, who obsessively tended his gardens. He was an ingenious gardener, a reclusive and timid man. Sometimes the priest, Mabeuf, came to see him. He was Gillenormand's son-in-law, Georges Pontmercy, an old soldier with a distinguished career. He accompanied Napoleon to Elba and fought at Waterloo. In 1815 his wife died, leaving a child named Marius, M. Gillenormand's grandson. Gillenormand claimed Marius and Pontmercy transferred his love to his flowers. Gillenormand ignored him. Occasionally Pontmercy would visit Paris and secretly watch his son who was the heir to his aunt Gillenormand's fortune. It became known – the priest in Paris was a brother to the priest in Vernon, M. Mabeuf. Occasionally Marius wrote to his father – Pontmercy wrote affectionate letters back but Gillenormand intercepted them and Marius did not see them.

Chapter 3

What Marius Pontmercy knows of the world he has learned through Baronne de T.'s salon and that brought him little happiness. Most of the members of the salon were haughty, elderly and from a noble background. One of the salon members, during the Revolution, had been put in the galleys at Toulon.
Marius, a royalist, received a good education and after college went to law school. He has little love for his grandfather.

Chapter 4

Before Marius entered law school his grandfather moved to Mardis; they did not return to the salon. In 1827, when Marius was sixteen, his grandfather tells him he is to go to see his father in Vernon. Marius is convinced that his father does not love him. When he arrives he finds his father dead, having sent for him during a recent illness. Marius does not grieve – he hardly knew his father who has left a note in which he mentions an innkeeper named Thenardier who saved his life at Waterloo. Marius soon returns to Paris, back to his law studies.

Chapter 5

Marius goes to mass at Saint-Sulpice and inadvertently takes M. Mabeuf's seat. Mabeuf tells him the story of a Waterloo veteran, kept from his son by his father-in-law, who would come to the church just to see his son. It was Pontmercy.
Marius tells his grandfather he wants to go away for three days.

Chapter 6

Marius returns after three days and then reads all he can about France's recent history, including his father's military history. He continues to study law and hardly sees his Gillenormand relatives. He is gradually beginning to think differently about the Republic and the Empire. He becomes an ardent supporter of Napoleon and less tolerant of his grandfather, although he shows nothing of this on the surface.
From time to time he goes to Montfermeil to look for Thenardier, the man who saved his father.

Chapter 7

Lieutenant Theodule Gillenormand, a fine officer, is a great-grand nephew of M. Gillenormand. Marius has never met this cousin.
One evening M. Gillenormand tells his daughter that Marius is going away again. She is curious about where he goes. The same night Theodule makes a surprise visit on his way through Paris. His aunt suggests he follow Marius and he follows him to his father's grave in Vernon.

Chapter 8

Theodule has respect for Marius's visiting the grave of the Colonel, but does not tell his aunt where Marius goes. Marius returns home and leaves his medal on its black ribbon on his bed. Inside the medal they find a note. The note is from Marius's father and in it he transfers his title of Baron to his son. The Gillenormands find Marius's business cards with his new title on them – Le Baron Marius Pontmercy. When Marius returns he and his grandfather have a heated argument about Marius's father. Marius denigrates the monarchy. His grandfather throws him out.

Book 4

Chapter 1

Political change is in the air in France; people were changing alliances and embracing new ideas. In Paris there was a small organization called the Friends of the ABC. These men are the friends of the poor and are interested in improving their education. Most of them are students – one is Enjolras, a handsome, charming and wealthy twenty-two year old man and an idealist who is extremely well-read. The men are all quite different to one another but all desire one thing – Progress. Enjolras's biggest supporter in the group is Grantaire.

Chapter 2

One of the young men of ABC, Laigle, sees a cabiolet passing by the Cafe Musain one day. The luggage in the cab reads "Marius Pontmercy". The carriage stops and Laigle tells Marius he has been looking for him. He says he does not know him but knows he was absent from law school the day before when roll was called. Laigle pretended to be Pontmercy and answered the roll call. Another of the ABC, Courfeyrac, comes out and Pontmercy, who has nowhere to stay, goes with him to a hotel.

Chapter 3

Marius became friends with Courfeyrac who did not ask him nosey questions. Within a few days he asks Marius if he has any political opinions. Marius says he is a democrat-Bonapartist. Courfeyrac takes him to a meeting of the ABC. He listens to the young men discuss every subject under the sun.

Chapter 4

One winter evening at the Cafe Musain the ABC are talking of this and that. Grantaire goes into a rant and condemns the whole world, saying he needs a drink. Some of the men are writing a vaudeville performance. Two of them are playing dominoes and talking of love and their mistresses. At another table mythology is being discussed. A copy of the charter of Louis XVIII is thrown in the fire.

Chapter 5

Courfeyrac begins to speak about Waterloo; Marius pays attention. He stands up and speaks in support of Napoleon Bonaparte. He considers Napoleon a genius. He asks what better thing there could be than the glory of France. One of the men answers "to be free". Everyone leaves, except Enjolras.

Chapter 6

Marius returns home, profoundly shaken. He is not sure how to handle his transition from a Royalist to a democrat. He stopped going to the Cafe Musain. The hotel owner is demanding his payment. Marius tells Courfeyrac that he is alone in the world and is poor. He sells his watch and most of his clothing; most of the proceeds go to paying the hotel bill. He soon receives six hundred francs from his aunt, which he returns to her. He leaves the hotel.

Book 5

Chapter 1

Marius sinks into poverty. He does not have enough to eat, or money to pay rent. His pride disappears and he lives without love. His aunt sends money, which he returns. He allows Courfeyrac to give him an old coat. He continues his studies and is admitted as a lawyer. Marius writes and tells his grandfather who throws the letter away.

Chapter 2

Marius adjusts to his poverty as well as he can and by working hard, he is able to scrape by. He learned German and English so he can translate for a publisher Courfeyrac knows. He lives in the Gorbeau "hovel", paying a low rent, and has a housekeeper who performs light duties. He eats little. His life is simple but he is not in debt. Marius is still concerned about Thenardier who he heard has fallen on hard times. He has looked for him for three years, without success.

Chapter 3

Marius is now twenty. He has not seen his grandfather in three years. He believes his grandfather does not love him, but he is wrong. His grandfather regrets his actions and misses Marius. Marius is not bitter but he rarely thinks of Gillenormand; he is more attached to the memory of his father. Marius has turned to a life of contemplation, perhaps a little too much so. He is offered a better place to live and an increase in salary, but refuses it, afraid to lose his freedom. He has three friends: Enjolras, Courfeyrac, and M. Mabeuf.

Chapter 4

Marius considers M. Mabeuf, as old as he is, his best friend. Mabeuf is apolitical – he loves books and his garden, as Marius's father did. He loves church as it is the only place men are quiet. He has written a book on flowers and still draws royalties from it. But Mabeuf is falling upon hard times.

Chapter 5

Time passes. Marius sees Mabeuf twice a month. He spends much time alone, walking or visiting the market. At the Gorbeau house he was known as M. Marius. He has been to see some of his father's old friends. He still held the same opinions but is not as passionate about them. In 1831 his housekeeper tells him his neighbors the Jondrettes have been turned out as they did not pay their rent – Marius gives his housekeeper money for them and tells her not to tell them it was his.

Chapter 6

The officer Theodule comes to visit his Gillenormand relatives again. Mlle Gillenormand wants him to replace Marius in his grandfather's heart. She advises Theodule to agree to anything his great-great uncle says. Gillenormand is raging about students gathering to protest. Theodule agrees with him but his uncle calls him a fool.

Book 6

Chapter 1

Marius is a handsome young man of medium height. He is reserved and not very friendly, with a severe look but a beautiful smile. He believes that he is unattractive to women and h is basically afraid of them. His friends encourage him to find a girlfriend. There is one female he notices – a young girl who sits on a bench in the Luxembourg garden with a much older man, perhaps her father. At first Marius is not very impressed with her.

Chapter 2

One day, many months later, Marius sees the man and girl on the bench again. The girl has changed; Marius now sees she is tall and beautiful, about fifteen years old. She is dressed in a more adult manner. She looks at Marius with little interest as he passes back and forth several times.

Chapter 3

One day the glances of Marius and the girl meet. There is an instant attraction between the two. Marius chides himself for not dressing better.

Chapter 4

The next day Marius puts on some new clothes and sets off for the Luxembourg. He meets Courfeyrac, ignores him, and his friend tells the others that Marius looks very stupid. Marius sees the man he secretly calls M. Leblanc with the young woman, sitting on "their bench". He walks by the bench but does not speak to them.

Chapter 5

The housekeeper at the Gorbeau hovel is Madame Burgon. She is surprised to see Marius put on his best clothes to go out three days in a row. Marius goes to Luxembourg again and repeats his trips for the next two weeks.

Chapter 6

Toward the end of the second week Marius was on his bench, pretending to read a book. Suddenly "M. Leblanc" and the girl are walking toward him. As they pass the girl gazes at him. Marius is overcome and walks around the Luxembourg garden "like a madman". Marius is falling in love with the mysterious girl.

Chapter 7

Marius has a passionate nature and is obsessed with the girl. He returns to the Luxembourg and sees her, but does not speak. He takes a handkerchief left on "M. Leblanc's" bench with the letter "U" embroidered on it – he decides that the girl's name is Ursule. He keeps the handkerchief, kissing it and laying it next to his heart.

Chapter 8

Marius is upset one day when the wind blows the girl's skirt up and he is jealous that someone else might have seen her legs. He gives her a "sullen and ferocious glance" and she looks puzzled. It took him three days to forgive "Ursule" her transgression.

Chapter 9

Marius decides he wants to know where "Ursule" lives. He follows her home to her modest three story house in Rue de l'Ouest. He asks the porter in the building about "M. Leblanc"; he tells him the man is not wealthy, but does much for the poor. The next day, when he follows them, "M. Leblanc" gave me a long hard look. For the next week the man and girl don't appear at Luxembourg. The porter at their house tells him they have moved out.

Book 7

Chapter 1

The lowest level of society is like the lowest depths of a mine. They have no interest in the progress of the universe.

Chapter 2

Those in the lowest mines have two mothers – ignorance and misery. Their guide is necessity, and their satisfaction is appetite. In the upper mine is Progress. It is time to look in the "cavern of evil".

Chapter 3

The "third lower floor" of Paris is governed by four ruffians from 1830-35: Gueulemer, Babet, Claquesous and Montparnasse. Gueulemer is a huge strong man but not very bright. Babet is slightly built and intelligent. He calls himself a Dental Artist. Claquesous only appears at night. He is a ventriloquist. Montparnasse is less than twenty years old and handsome. He commits robberies with violence and is a killer.

Chapter 4

These four men work together, almost as one, "a mysterious robber with four heads". Their turf is the area near the Salpetriere. They call their gang the "Patron-Minette". There are a number of others from the low end of Paris society in their gang. These men have no morals, no consciences, and no scruples.

Book 8

Chapter 1

Marius has not seen M. Leblanc or the girl in Luxembourg garden for three seasons. He is desperate to see her again. He finds no joy in social occasions and spends more and more time alone. One day he meets a man who bears a strong resemblance to Leblanc.

Chapter 2

Marius is still living at the Gorbeau house. He pays no attention to the others living there, including the Jondrettes. One day he goes out and sees two girls in rags. He hears them talking about the police coming for them. He finds some papers they have dropped but cannot locate the girls.

Chapter 3

Later on, one night, he finds the papers in the pocket. He opens the envelope and finds four unsealed letters. They smell of tobacco and are all begging for monetary help although signed with different names. No addresses of the writers are included and all are written in the same writing on the same type of paper. He throws them in a corner of his room. Not long after a man and a girl appear at his door.

Chapter 4

The girl looks unhealthy and is dressed in rags. She is fifteen going on fifty and was once pretty. She gives him a letter from her father, Jondrette. They are the tenants Marius had paid the rent for six months before. The letter is begging for food; Jondrette's wife is ill. Marius recognizes the writing as matching the four he found earlier. He understands now – that Jondrette will use any means to alleviate his family's plight. Meanwhile the girl is roaming around his room, looking at everything. She grabs a book and begins to read – it mentions Waterloo and she says her father was there. She shows him she can write and then begins to flirt with him. Marius steps back and then gives her the envelope of letters he found. She tells him about their miserable life; he gives her most of the money he has.

Chapter 5

Marius has lived five years in poverty but knows there are some worse off. The young girl has opened his eyes. He feels guilty for ignoring his neighbors, the Jondrettes. He decides to get to know them. He looks through a peephole into their apartment.

Chapter 6

Marius's apartment is modest, theirs is squalid. They have few possessions. Wood-lice and spiders share their space. He can see a small man about sixty years old, a "hideous scoundrel". He is writing. Nearby is a tall woman of indeterminate age. A young girl who looks eleven or twelve is lying on a pallet.

Chapter 7

Marius is just about to turn away when the girl who came to his apartment earlier, returns home. She announces "he" is coming – the "philanthropist" – meaning a man she has seen at church. She has given him one of the begging letters. The man orders the other girl to break a pane of glass and his wife to pretend to be ill. He wants the "philanthropist" to feel pity for them.

Chapter 8

Marius continues to watch the Jondrettes. The man is getting impatient for the philanthropist to arrive. He begins to rant about wealthy people. A knock comes at the door: the man changes his demeanor when he lets the philanthropist in. The new arrival – it is M. Leblanc - has a girl with him. The girl Marius is in love with.

Chapter 9

Marius is overcome on seeing her. He watches Jondrette bow down to the earth floor telling the man his name is Fabantou – he lists their problems (some are lies). He pinches his younger daughter so she will cry. He whispers to his wife to take a close look at the man. The philanthropist gives him five francs but promises to return with more money that evening. He gives his coat to Jondrette.

Chapter 10

While Marius looked through the peephole he was watching the young girl, his "Ursule". She has clothing and blankets for the Jondrettes. He decides to follow her when they leave but their carriage gets a head start. On the street he does not notice Jondrette talking to a group of policemen.

Chapter 11

Marius goes back into the building; the elder Jondrette girl follows him. When he reaches his room she grabs the door as he enters. He asks her what she wants and she asks him what is wrong and offers to help him. He wants to know the address of the philanthropist. She says she will get it and leaves. Marius hears the voice of Jondrette saying that "I recognized him" and thinks he is referring to M. Leblanc. He goes back to his peep-hole.

Chapter 12

Jondrette is telling his wife that after eight years, he recognizes the man. He yells at his daughters to leave the hovel. When they do, he tells his wife the young lady with M. Leblanc is "she". His wife is enraged. He tells her his fortune is made and for her to wait and see what happens when Leblanc arrives at six that evening. Jondrette goes out on a secret errand. It is one o'clock.

Chapter 13

Marius decides that Jondrette is up to no good and must be stopped. He does not know Leblanc's address but decides to go out. He comes across two men on the other side of a wall, talking in low tones. He thinks they have something to do with Jondrette. He heads to a police station.

Chapter 14

Marius arrives at the police station on Rue de Pontoise. He is sent to speak to an inspector. He tells him his story; the inspector thinks the Patron-Minette must have a hand in this. Marius tells him about the two men he overheard. He gives his inspector the pass-key to the house and he is given two small pistols with which warn the police outside of what is going on. As Marius leaves the inspector tells him his name is Javert.

Chapter 15

Courfeyrac and Bossuet see Marius walking along the road. Courfeyrac says they should ignore him that it looks like he is following someone (it is Jondrette). They decide to follow Marius. Jondrette completes several mysterious errands and then Marius realizes he must go home before the housekeeper locks the outer door. Marius is soon back in his room, seen by no-one.

Chapter 16

It is almost six o'clock. Marius can see a light in the Jondrettes' apartment through his peephole. When Jondrette arrives home Marius listens to their conversation. Madame says Marius has been out all day and one of the daughters comes into Marius's chamber – he has been able to conceal himself under the bed. She does not look there. Jondrette sends his daughters out to stand guard.

Chapter 17

Marius returns to his peephole. He can see piles of iron and ropes near a roaring fire in the brazier. Jondrette is smoking his pipe and his wife is speaking quietly. Suddenly the woman comes into Marius's apartment to borrow two chairs. She does not see Marius standing on the commode. She returns to her apartment and Jondrette sends her outside. Marius sees Jondrette take out a knife. The young man readies one of the pistols.

Chapter 18

The church clock strikes six o'clock. M. Leblanc appears in the Jondrette's apartment. He gives Jondrette some money. Madame Jondrette goes downstairs to dismiss the carriage and M. Leblanc sits down with Jondrette. Marius watches every movement.

Chapter 19

Leblanc asks Jondrette about his daughters. Madame has returned and Leblanc comments that Madame "Fabantou" appears to be better. Jondrette replies that she is dying. They chat briefly. Suddenly a man enters the room very quietly – Marius and Leblanc notice him at the same time. Jondrette says he is a neighbor. Then another man enters. They sit on a bed behind Jondrette. Two more men come in. Their faces are blackened; Jondrette says they are chimney builders. Feeling uneasy, Leblanc stands up. Jondrette talks on and then asks Leblanc if he recognizes him.

Chapter 20

The garret door has opened and three more men appear. Jondrette asks them a number of questions. Leblanc is pale; he knows he has fallen into a trap. Three of the men block the doorway. Leblanc says he does not recognize Jondrette who tells him he is Thenardier, the inn-keeper of Montfermeil. Marius is shocked to hear Jondrette speak his real name. He is the man who had saved his father's life. Thenardier harangues Leblanc, calling him a child-stealer. The man denies everything and calls Thenardier a villain. Thenardier demands a large amount of money. Thenardier turns his back to speak to one of the other men and Leblanc overturns a chair and the table; he is half out the window when he is attacked and dragged back. They search him for money and valuables then throw him on a pallet and tie him up. Thenardier demands two hundred thousand francs. He unties his right arm and orders him to write what he will dictate - a note to Cosette by her old nickname "Lark". Leblanc pretends not to know who he means but writes the note and signs it Urbain Fabre.

Thenardier sends his wife and one of the thugs out with the note. There are five men left in the apartment with Leblanc and Thenardier. The men are wearing disguises of one sort or another. Thenardier waits for his wife to return.

Marius wonders who "Lark" is, if she is "Ursule". He remains at his peephole, mesmerized by what he has witnessed. All is quiet for awhile and then Thenardier tells Leblanc that Lark is being taken for ransom. Leblanc will have to pay two hundred thousand francs to get her back. Marius is stunned. He does not know if he should alert the police.

Madame Thenardier returns and says Leblanc gave them a false address. Marius is relieved – "Ursule" is safe. Leblanc suddenly stands up and grabs a hot chisel out of the brazier. He has freed his hands and one leg. He burns his own flesh with the chisel which he then throws out of the window and tells the men to do whatever they want with him. The men want to kill him and the only question is how.

Marius tosses a note into the next apartment saying the police are coming. The men decide it is time to leave, going through their only window with a rope ladder. Before they can organize themselves Javert is at the door.

Chapter 21

Before arriving at the Thenardier's, Javert had seized Azelma but Eponine eluded him. He grew impatient waiting for Marius's pistol shot and went upstairs. He had Marius's key, was able to go in, arriving in the nick of time. The men throw themselves at him, as though they are the victims. Thenardier shoots, but his gun misfires. Madame Thenardier throws a large stone at Javert. Finally everyone is rounded up and arrested. Leblanc has escaped out the window.

Chapter 22

A small lad is walking in the direction of the Barriere de Fontainebleau. He comes across an old woman rummaging through garbage. He is rude to her. He goes up to the Gorbeau hovel and bangs and kicks on the door. She recognizes him as Thenardier's son and happily tells him his family is in jail.

Volume 4

Book 1

Chapter 1

The Restoration of 1814 had led to almost immediate French dissatisfaction with the Bourbons. The people wanted peace but the politicians wanted greatness. A series of uprisings led to a revolution in July of 1830 which resulted in downfall of the Bourbons.

Chapter 2

The Revolution of 1830 "is a revolution arrested midway". The bourgeoisie were happy with less than the power-hungry; the latter wanted more from the Revolution. The years following 1830 until 1848 can be called the "halt" when there was not great change and there was a return to the monarchy in the person of Louis Philippe.

Chapter 3 and 4

Louis Philippe was a good man of good character and he possessed the skills to rule well. His character and his actions were of moderation and he was charming. He did not behave like a man of privilege and the bourgeoisie loved him for that. Louis Philippe did not seek glory for France and he alienated many.

Chapter 5

Unhappiness with Louis Philippe leads to discontent. The French people wanted to rule themselves; they are fed up with monarchy. Change is plotted quietly and the numbers wanting change grows steadily. But it is not despotism or terrorism the people want.

Chapter 6

The young men, now older, of the ABC, are having a secret meeting at the Cafe Musain. They are in support of change and must organize themselves to engage the people. Enjolras directs their game plan. Grantaire, never very serious, wants to play his part. Enjolras tells him to stay out of it but then consents and tells him to go to the Barriere du Maine. The other men are assigned their tasks. Later Enjolras checks out what Grantaire is doing. He goes to the Richefeu and finds Grantaire in an argument with another man – they are playing dominoes.

Book 2

Chapter 1

After Javert arrests the Thenardiers and their accomplices Marius leaves the house and goes to see Courfeyrac. His friend is living in an area of town where political dissidents congregate. He spends the night there and the next morning goes home, pays the rent he owes, and moves out without leaving his new address. Javert tries to find him but cannot. Marius spends a couple of months with Courfeyrac. He is in muddle of unhappiness. He is unsure of Leblanc, misses "Ursule", know known to him as Lark, and again lives in poverty. When he discovers the meadow of the Lark, he returns daily, thinking he will find his love there.

Chapter 2

Javert was very disappointed that he had not been able to take "Leblanc" prisoner. One of Thenardier's colleagues, Montparnasse, had also escaped arrest. Thenardier's daughter, Eponine had been captured and joined her sister Azelma at the women's prison. He had also let Claquesous slip through his hands. He still wants to find Marius, although he can't remember his name.
In prison a series of communications reached Eponine to which she replied that nothing would be done. This would have later repercussions.

Chapter 3

Marius sometimes saw Father Mabeuf. The latter is still gardening and eats very little; he is almost eighty years old. One day M. Mabeuf is in his garden. He tries to remove the top off the well to water his plants but cannot. Suddenly a young girl appears and offers to help. She watered his garden and then asks him where Marius lives. He tells her Marius often goes to the meadow of the Lark.

Chapter 4

Four days later, Marius, who anonymously gives money to Thenardier, goes to the Lark's meadow. He sees the elder of the Thenardier girls there. She is barefoot and in rags, but very pretty and happy to see Marius. Eponine tells him she was in jail for two weeks. She hints that he left the Gorbeau hovel due to the incident with her father and asks him where he now lives. He does not tell her but she informs him she knows where "Lark" lives. Marius tells not to give Thenardier the address. She begins to lead him there.

Book 3

Chapter 1

In 1829 a derelict house in the Rue Plumet was restored and taken by an older man with a young girl. There were no neighbors on this isolated street. The man was Jean Valjean and the girl Cosette. They had one elderly female servant, Toussaint. Valjean goes by the name of Fauchelevent. They left the convent because he decided Cosette had to see something of life. When old Fauchelevent died, Valjean received his inheritance. He adopted the name Ultime Fauchelevent.

Chapter 2

Valjean and Cosette live most of the time in Rue Plumet. There is a smaller house at the back of the property where Valjean stays. The property retains some of its earlier luxurious splendor. Valjean and Cosette go for a walk each day, visiting the poor and the sick. They always leave by the door on Rue de Babylone. Valjean is now sixty years old and still fulfills his military duty in the National Guard.

Chapter 3

The garden at Valjean's is extraordinary. People stop to admire it and to wonder what is behind the gates of the property. It is an uncultivated garden and has run wild and hundreds of butterflies fly about. The statues and steps are crumbling.

Chapter 4

The garden, with hidden arbors and grottos, had originally been planted to hide a mistress's house, built by a chief justice. It had now returned to a virginal and modest state. In this garden is a heart waiting for love – it belongs to Cosette. She was fourteen when she left the convent and had no mother to form her soul. Valjean was an old man and could not fill that role, although he had other wisdom to impart. She has no memories of Fantine and only vague ones of her early childhood with the Thenardiers. Valjean told her nothing of her mother.

Chapter 5

Cosette discovers a mirror and begins to believe she might be pretty. She begins to spend more time in the front garden, where she will be noticed. After a lapse of six months, she and Marius see each other again at the Luxembourg.

Chapter 6

Destiny brings Cosette and Marius together. They have already been drawn together at their first glance. The two of them experience the deification of the stranger – the unknown turned into perfection.

Chapter 7

Valjean becomes aware of Marius who avoids "the father". Valjean "cordially detested" the young man but said nothing to Cosette about him until one day he comments on his "pedantic air". Valjean thinks Marius is in love with Cosette but that she has not even noticed him. He does not trust Marius and does not want to lose Cosette. He moves them away from the area and they do not visit the Luxembourg for months. Cosette is suffering but she does not let Valjean know.

Chapter 8

Valjean does not want to lose Cosette. He knows he is being childish but can't help it. They continue their early morning walks, sometimes to an area of wild meadows. One morning they go to the Barriere du Maine. A group of carts and men appear. There are seven wagons with a couple of dozen men on each one. Valjean looks terrified and Cosette is frightened, but for a different reason. He tells her they are convicts heading to the galleys. Cosette is very upset for the rest of the day.

Book 4

Chapter 1

Valjean and Cosette still visit the poor and take them food and clothing. One of these trips is to the Jondrette apartment. The next day Valjean appears with a large wound on his arm that looked like a burn. It becomes infected and he has fever for a month. Cosette nurses him. His happiness returns and he almost forgets what had happened with the Thenardiers. He assumes they are in prison. Cosette begins to stroll alone in their garden.

Chapter 2

Little Gavroche, wandering around the city, has come across Valjean and Cosette's home. One night he begins to climb the hedge to steal fruit. He hears voices of an old man seated on a bench – an old woman is standing, addressing him as M. Mabeuf. She is Madame Plutarque. They are discussing needing money to pay the rent. Gavroche hides in the hedge and soon two more people appear. One of them is the ruffian Montparnasse. He attacks the man who overpowers him. He asks Montparnasse what his ambition is – he replies "a thief". The older man warns him of the perils of such a life. In the end he gives Montparnasse his money and he leaves. Gavroche attacks Montparnasse and retrieves Valjean's wallet (for it is Valjean) and throws it back over the hedge to the old man. Madame Plutarque states that it fell from heaven.

Book 5

Chapter 1

Cosette realizes that she has not thought about Marius in quite some time. A couple of days in a row she sees a handsome young officer passing by. After that, he passes by almost every day. It is Theodule Gillenormand. Meanwhile Marius is deeply depressed about Cosette.

Chapter 2

Jean Valjean occasionally goes away by himself. During the first half of April, he did this and not even Cosette knows where he is. Cosette is playing the piano-organ the night of his departure and hears footsteps in the garden; she looks and sees no-one there. The next evening, at dusk, she thinks she hears footsteps again. She sees a shadow in the moonlight – a shadow of a man in a round hat, which soon disappears. Valjean returns the next day and checks the gate. The next two nights he prowls around the garden realizes it was the neighbor's chimney-pipe which had created the shadow. Cosette relaxes once more.

Chapter 3

Not long after this Cosette is walking around the garden. When she returns to her favorite bench there is a stone on the seat. She asks Toussaint if her father, who went out, is back. Cosette expresses her nervousness about their security. When she wakes at sunrise she laughs at herself for being scared and goes outside and looks under the stone – there is an unsealed envelope.

Chapter 4

God is behind everything, but everything hides God. Some thoughts are prayers. The future belongs to the heart, more than the mind. This is the nature of love. God does not add to love, but He adds to duration. Without love the soul suffocates. It is grander to love than to be loved.

Chapter 5

Cosette finishes reading the fifteen-page letter left under the stone and the officer walks by as usual. She now thinks he is hideous. The letter has awakened love and destiny in her. There is no name or address on it but she thinks it is from Marius. The officer walks by again – she glances up and he smiles. She feels like throwing something at him. Inside the house she gives in to a confusion of joy and fear.

Chapter 6

That evening Valjean goes out; Cosette dresses up and goes out to sit on the garden bench. She senses someone is behind her and looks up to see Marius. She tries to hide behind a tree but soon he begins to talk and declares his love for her. She eventually does the same and they kiss, and talk. And finally, they tell each other their names.

Book 6

Chapter 1

The Thenardiers have a total of five children: two girls, then three boys. Madame detested her sons and loves only her daughters. The couple contrived to be rid of their two youngest sons. Magnon, the woman who had blackmailed old Gillenormand over the birth of her boys lost her two sons to illness. Magnon received eighty francs a month for her sons and could not afford the loss. She made a deal with the Thenardiers for their sons who were the same age. The couple would get part of the amount Gillenormand paid each month and they changed their name to Jondrette. Magnon was taken to jail one day and the boys were left behind, homeless.

Chapter 2

The spring of 1832 is very cold. Little Gavroche is standing in front of a wig shop. He is hoping to steal a bar of soap to sell for a sou. Two boys younger than him, about five and seven, enter the shop and the barber throws them out. Gavroche talks to them; they do not have a place to sleep. He tells them to come with him and buys them all some bread. He finds Montparnasse and it is obvious from the conversation Gavroche knows something of the criminal world. Gavroche takes the children to sleep in a monument of an elephant, near the Bastille. He tells the boys he will take care of them from now on. Later that night Montparnasse comes for Gavroche.

Chapter 3

A jailbreak is planned for Brujon, Guelener and Thenardier (who is in solitary confinement), with Babet and Montparnasse's help from "outside". Brujon and Guelener escape the same night Gavroche meets the little boys. The next stage of the plan is to help Thenardier get out and his escape is hampered because the rope they have is too short. He is stuck and suddenly there is an uproar as the earlier escape is discovered. Thenardier can hear the escapees, along with Montparnasse, talking below him. He drops the rope to them and they decide they need a child to climb it. Gavroche is fetched and when he goes up he recognizes his father. When the man is safe on the ground, Gavroche leaves.

Book 7

Chapters 1-4

Slang is the language of the people – a nation and a dialect. Purists who don't approve of slang avoid the exploration of all society. It may not be attractive to explore the lower level but it is necessary to understand the whole society. Slang comes out of wretchedness and is a shield against those who make the wretched miserable. Slang is a dressing-room where the language, having something to hide, dresses itself. It has its syntax and its poetry. It is a language within a language and worthy of study. All the main European languages have slang. Slang can express joy and it can express sorrow and all emotions in between. Slang can be created during a period in of great change and unrest, such as Jacquerie.

Book 8

Chapter 1

Eponine has kept the ruffians away from Marius, whom she adores. Marius is spending much time with his beloved, Cosette. The garden is a sheltered private place, where they meet during May, 1832. They pass their time talking and teasing, complimenting each other, in adoration.

Chapter 2

The couple has not revealed much of their past to each other. Marius does not tell her about the incident in the Thenardiers' apartment when her father was held captive and then escaped. Loving and thinking do not always go together.

Chapter 3

Cosette was happy, which pleased Jean Valjean. He is unaware of her relationship with Marius and Cosette wants to keep it that way. Toussaint knows nothing – she goes to bed early and Marius visits after ten at night. Marius's friend, Courfeyrac, teases him about his irregular hours; Marius refuses to tell him about Cosette. One night on his way to see her he runs into Eponine. He has nothing to say to her and she leaves, disappointed.

Chapter 4

On the 3rd of June, 1832, the next night, Marius sees Eponine in the distance. He changes his route but she follows him, not knowing where he is going. She hides herself in a nook outside Cosette's garden. It is almost ten o'clock and six men appear in the street and halt at Valjean's gate. They begin to break in and Eponine warns them of a dog in the yard. Her father is one of the men and his usual gang members are with him. Eponine has not seen him since his jailbreak and pretends to be welcoming him back. She tells the men the house is empty. They don't believe her and she threatens to call the police and to scream. Finally, the men leave.

Chapter 5

The Rue Plumet goes back to its peaceful tranquility once the men have gone, only the trees a witness to what has happened.

Chapter 6

———

Eponine remains at the gate, and Marius is in the garden with Cosette. He has never been happier but when he sees Cosette, he can see she's been weeping. She tells him Valjean has told her they may go to England. Marius cannot imagine giving Cosette up. She says she will have to go but that Marius could come with them. He says he cannot, he has no money but if she leaves, he will die. He says he has something to do and will return in two nights. He gives her his address.

Chapter 7

M. Gillenormand has passed his ninety-first birthday and has slowed down slightly. He misses Marius – he has not seen him for four years and wants to see him before he dies. His daughter's attempt to replace Marius with Theodule has not worked out. One day Marius shows up and Gillenormand is pleased to see him, but he cannot show his happiness due to pride. Marius tells him he wants permission to marry. At first Gillenormand refuses and then orders Marius to tell him about it, his heart softened by Marius calling him "father". Gillenormand quickly realizes that Cosette is the girl Theodule has told him about and tells Marius to make her just his mistress. Insulted, Marius leaves.

Book 9

Chapter 1

Valjean is sitting alone in the Champ-de-Mars. Valjean has decided to go to England, to protect both Cosette and himself.

One morning, in the garden, he comes across an address, scratched on the wall (it is Marius's address). He is worried, not knowing what it means.

As he sits, a note falls into his lap – on it is a warning that he should move out of his house. He sees someone running away, no bigger than a child.

Chapter 2

Marius is in despair and wanders the streets until two a.m. In the morning he goes out, with the two loaded pistols Javert had given him in February. He wanders around all day. That night he goes to Rue Plumet but Cosette is not in her usual spot. He knocks on the door but there is no answer. He hears a voice, like Eponine's, but rougher and deeper, telling him his friends are in Rue de la Chanvrerie

Chapter 3

Mabeuf has handed in what is Valjean's purse, thrown over the hedge by Gavroche, to the police. Mabeuf is becoming poorer – the plates for his books on flowers are gone so he can no longer make copies. He neglects his garden and lives on bread and potatoes. He has sold most of his possessions, except for his most treasured books. When he begins to sell these, all hope seems lost.

On June 4th he hears shots and is told there are riots.

Book 10

Chapter 1

A revolt has begun. It is not truly an uprising and does not have the great consequences of Bastille Day, July 14th. But what was the cause of this uprising?

Chapter 2

How does one define an uprising as opposed to an insurrection? The former is in the right, the latter in the wrong. It all depends on which side one is on. Insurrections are often more violent, more heated but they all begin with riots. Was the movement of June 1832 a revolt or an insurrection? It is a matter of opinion.

Chapter 3

Paris had been in the grip of a cholera epidemic in the spring of 1832 but it was ripe for a "commotion". The death of Colonel Lamarque set it off; he had served under Napoleon. He was a French patriot. The people of Faubourg Saint-Antoine are armed the day of his funeral. Some are planning an insurrection. The government sends armed troops into the streets. The funeral procession grows and when it reaches the Bastille, the throng from Faubourg Saint-Antoine, a "seething" begins to take place. Sometime later shots are discharged and the riots begin.

Chapter 4

The riot was expected but chaos rules. Within fifteen minutes the city is in an uproar. Partisan groups display their colors and their weapons. Arms factories are looted and guns seized. Private dwellings are entered and weapons taken. Students aid in the uprising and help erect barricades. The rioters control a third of the city. The National Guard begins to fire on the people; deaths occur on both sides.

Chapter 5

This was not the first insurrection to take place in Paris in recent years but the city took them in stride. This time it is different as it is more serious. The government makes plans to overthrow the insurrection using the force of the army and there is criticism when it does not happen quickly. The theatres stayed closed and hundreds are arrested. The people wait for the first cannon-shot. They barricade themselves inside their homes.

Book 11

Chapter 1

Gavroche is wandering through the city during the riots. He has an old holster-pistol he grabbed from a shop. He waves the pistol in the air and sings a battle song. Eventually he realizes the pistol has no trigger.

A few months before, Gavroche had left the two little boys who shared his elephant shelter to their fate, after getting them a breakfast of sorts. They were supposed to meet him at the same spot later. They never return.

Gavroche continues his way through the city, vandalizing theatre posters and insulting the rich men he encounters.

Chapter 2

Gavroche comes across four elderly women, poverty stricken and decrepit. He asks them why they speak of politics and they call him a rascal, a beggar's brat. He thumbs his nose at them. They see his pistol and tell him he is headed for the guillotine.

Chapter 3

A barber is shaving an old solder and asks him about Napoleon – what he was like as a rider, what his horses had been like, if he had been wounded. Suddenly a cannon-ball hits the shop and a stone is thrown through the window – by Gavroche. It is the shop from where the two little boys had been chased away twelve weeks before.

Chapter 4

Gavroche joins a group of men that include Enjolras, Courfeyrac, and other friends of Marius. They have some unusual weapons. As they proceed, one of them pulls down a notice from the Archbishop allowing his "flock" to eat eggs during Lent. He is enraged that people can be told what to eat.

Their numbers swell as they march. Mabeuf joins them, though he is carrying no weapon.

Chapter 5

Courfeyrac recognizes Mabeuf from walking with Marius by his door. The old man seems disoriented and Courfeyrac tells him he should go home, that there is going to be a "row"; that they are going to overthrow the government. He joins them anyway. Gavroche is leading them all, loudly singing a folk song.

Chapter 6

Near the Rue des Billettes, a stranger, a tall middle-aged man joins them. Gavroche continues his wild running and singing and banging his pistol. Courfeyrac runs into his lodgings as they pass by – the portress tells him someone is waiting for him. At the same time a young female comes looking for Marius, who is not there. She asks Courfeyrac is she can join him – he has no objection.

Book 12

Chapter 1

There is a public house, Corinthe, at Rue de la Chanvrerie, where a barricade is erected during the riots. The street in a warren of streets, alleys lined with eight-story buildings, dirty and crowded. The Corinthe had deteriorated in recent years, due to the death of its recent proprietor, Hucheloup, and is run by his widow.

Chapter 2

On June 5th Laigle and Joly go to the Corinthe for breakfast. They have wine and oysters. Soon they are joined by Grantaire; more wine appears. They discuss the marching protestors, but Grantaire does not care; his only reality is drink and the rioters are imbeciles. They begin to talk about Marius's love affair. Suddenly a small boy appears, with a message from a "tall blonde fellow" – 'ABC'. They say it must come from Enjolras – but they decide to remain in the pub and get very drunk. Hours later they see the marchers through the door – Enjolras, Gavroche, and the others. They begin to build a barricade.

Chapter 3

The neighborhood around the Corinthe is under siege, its residents terrified. The pub is still open, drawing in crowds. Iron bars are wrenched out of the grated front and a dray cart is overturned. Stones are pulled up from the street, and more barrels from the cart and the pub cellar are used to barricade the road. An omnibus and horses are seized to further block the street. Grantaire is extremely drunk and Enjolras orders him away – but he falls asleep on the pub table.

Chapter 4

The rain finally stops and recruits arrive, along with gunpowder and weapons. The only street light is smashed. Courfeyrac, Combeferre and Enjolras direct everything. Many of the men have guns. Gavroche is still there, in the thick of it all, demanding a real gun to replace his broken one.

Chapter 5

The large barricade is built to a height of six or seven feet. It is built so the men can easily get behind it. The smaller barricade is erected behind the pub. One small area is left without a barricade, but the men believe it will be safe. A table is dragged out of the pub and Courfeyrac climbs on it to distribute cartridges for the men's guns.

Chapter 6

The men wait. They begin to recite love-verses about young love and spring. Stars are coming out now and lamps are lit. A flag had been raised earlier and light from a torch falls on it and enhances the scarlet color.

Chapter 7

The fifty men barricaded in the Rue de la Chanvrerie wait for the government troops to arrive. Gavroche is in the wine cellar with the man who had joined the insurgents in the Rue des Billettes. Enjolras finds Gavroche and tells him to slip out beyond the barricade and find out what is happening. Gavroche says the man in the wine cellar is a police spy. Enjolras gets some back-up and asks the man who he is and the man replies "Javert". They grab him, pin him down, search him and find his police identification. He is tied to a post in the middle of the cellar. Gavroche leaves on his mission.

Chapter 8

A man suggests they fire from a house that faces Rue Saint-Denis. He says they must break in and begins to batter the door with a gun. From a window above a porter refuses to open the door. The man aims the gun at him, but when the porter refuses again, he shoots him. Enjolras then kills the shooter and the body is thrown over the barricade. Enjolras announces to the crowd that he was killed for disobeying orders. Later, at the morgue, it is discovered the man, Cabuc, was an agent of the police.

Book 13

Chapter 1

Marius has almost arrived in the Rue de la Chanvrerie by a circuitous route through the city. He sees this as an opportunity to die, for he has nothing left to live for. He has Javert's pistols with him.

Chapter 2

The police shoot anywhere they see a candle – and sometimes kill. Paris is in the grip of horror. The battalions are still on the streets, slowly drawing in and around the insurrection.

Chapter 3

In the Rue de la Chanvrerie all is calm. Marius has only a little way to go; he is at the unguarded fragment of the Rue Mondetour. He sits upon a post and begins to think – about his father. Marius's day of battle had come; he was about to engage in civil war. He told Cosette that he would die if he could not be with her and now this may happen.

Book 14

Chapter 1

It is ten at night and the insurgents are still waiting inside the barricaded street, listening for the sound of marching. They hear Gavroche reciting poetry from Rue Saint-Denis, which contains a coded warning. The boy arrives, telling them the soldiers have come. Gavroche grabs Javert's gun. Footsteps approach – a challenge is issued and shots are fired; it appears to be a complete regiment. Enjolras challenges someone to plant a flag on the barricade.

Chapter 2

M. Mabeuf is still with the insurgents; he is in the pub. Others advise him to leave but he doesn't answer. When Enjolras makes his challenge, Mabeuf grabs the red banner and mounts the barricade. When he reaches the top he shouts "Long live the Republic" and is shot by the soldiers. Enjolras lauds Mabeuf's heroic action.

Chapter 3

Mabeuf's body is taken into the pub. The bearers taunt Javert as they pass by. Gavroche, outside, sounds a warning – municipal guards are breaking through the barricade. The insurgents begin firing and Gavroche tries to shoot Javert's gun but it is not loaded. A guard is just about to kill him when he is shot himself – by Marius.

Chapter 4

Marius has been shaken out of his reverie by seeing Mabeuf shot and Gavroche threatened. He gets rid of his pistols and just as he turns to look at a barrel of powder, a soldier takes aim. His arm is jostled by a young workman in velvet trousers and the ball does not hit him. He grabs the barrel of powder and threatens to blow up the whole barricade if the soldiers do not leave. The soldiers flee.

Chapter 5

The insurgents greet Marius with joy and gratitude. Marius is in a daze due to his anguish over Cosette and the death of Mabeuf, and the violence around him. He feels as though he is outside himself observing what is happening.

Beyond the barricade they hear the sounds of the soldiers, and then one of their own, Prouvaire, shouting and quickly silenced by a shot.

Chapter 6

Marius suddenly hears his name called – he recognizes Eponine's voice. She is dragging herself toward him, dressed in a pair of velvet pants – workmen's clothing. She is dying – her hand has a hole in it that she says was caused by her stopping a gun aimed at him. The ball went out through her back. She hears a boy singing and tells Marius it is her brother. She gives Marius a letter that she was supposed to mail him before and requests that he kiss her brow after she is dead. Just before Eponine dies she tells him she was a little in love with him.

Chapter 7

Marius kisses the dead girl's brow. He finds a quiet spot and reads the letter – it is from Cosette, telling him she and Valjean are going to England and includes the address where they now are. It had been Eponine who warned Valjean to leave and when Cosette wrote her note, she spied Eponine outside, now disguised in men's clothing. She took the note to give to Marius and ended up at the barricades, after asking Courfeyrac where Marius was. Marius is now overjoyed; Cosette does love him. He writes a note to her and tells Gavroche to deliver it.

Book 15

Chapter 1

Valjean, Cosette, and Toussaint are staying at Rue de l'Homme
Arme. For the first time he and Cosette had argued – over leaving
Rue Plumet. Valjean brought only his valise, always with him, to
their new address. The women bring very little. Once they arrive
Valjean relaxes but soon is in turmoil as he reads, in Cosette's
blotting book, the lines she had written to Marius. He is afraid of
losing her and plunges into grief. He assumes that the man she loves
is Marius. Toussaint told him there is fighting in the city and he asks
her where – and then he heads out.

Chapter 2

When Valjean goes out he can hear the faint sounds of the
insurgence. Soon he sees Gavroche, bringing the note from Marius.
The boy smashes a lantern and the street is darkened. Valjean,
knowing Gavroche is hungry, gives him a hundred sous. Gavroche
asks where No. 7 is and Valjean guesses he is bringing a note for
Cosette. The boy gives it to him and tells him he is returning to the
barricade.

Chapter 3

Valjean goes back to their new apartment, makes sure the women are
asleep, and reads the note – Marius writes to Cosette that he is going
to die. Valjean is initially happy. He puts on his old National Guard
uniform, which Toussaint had brought, and goes out. He takes a
gun.

Chapter 4

Gavroche heads back to the barricade, singing, pantomiming actions.
He comes across a carter asleep on the ground, with his head against
the cart. The boy pulls the cart away and leaves a note saying he has
taken the cart for the "French Republic". As he is moving the cart,
he comes face to face with a soldier. He manages to escape death
and heads off singing again, back to the barricade.

Volume 5

Book 1

Chapter 1

The lower classes can have a great influence on history – for instance "the rabble followed Jesus Christ".

Chapter 2

Later barricades in later insurrections would be superior to the one in Rue de la Chanvrerie but for the time it was formidable. Overnight, under the direction of Enjolras, it had been raised two feet. Rubbish and corpses have been removed, the uniforms of dead Guardsmen kept. Mabeuf's body is still in the tap-room and Javert is there tool, tied to his post. The men are tired, hungry, and sober.

Chapter 3

At six in the morning on June 6th Enjolras tells the men to prepare for an attack by the full force of the army and the National Guard. They will receive no help from the general population. Someone cries out that though the people have abandoned the republicans, they have not abandoned the people. The men cheer.

Chapter 4

The men discuss if some of them should leave – but there is no safe way to escape. Enjolras offers up the uniforms of the dead soldiers, but no one comes forward. He makes a speech about how their women and children will suffer if they die. Marius speaks up and agrees with Enjolras and finally five men agree to leave. There are only four uniforms – as they wrangle about who will stay another uniform appears – that of Jean Valjean's, who Marius recognizes as M. Fauchelevent. He had just arrived inside the barricade.

Chapter 5

Enjolras is standing on the barricade staircase made of paving stones – he gives a speech about the future they might have if their insurrection is successful. It is to rally his "troops" – for they are looking death in the face.

Chapter 6

Meanwhile, Marius is locked in his own thoughts – how did Fauchelevent, Cosette's father, come to be there? The man is ignoring Marius. Enjolras goes to Javert and gives him some water – the policeman asks if he could be tied to the top of the table rather than the post. He agrees and has his men tie him securely to the table.

Chapter 7

It is dawn. The height of the barricade has been increased. The last open spot on Mondetour lane has been barricaded. The men make ready for the attack. Enjolras takes his place and the men ready their guns. They did not wait for long – the soldiers arrive and Enjolras tells them to fire. Suddenly Gavroche appears inside the barricade. Cannon balls begin to descend on the insurgents.

Chapter 8

Marius asks Gavroche what he is doing there and the boy asks him the same. Gavroche tells Marius he delivered the letter to Cosette to the porter in their building. Marius asks the boy if he knows M. Fauchelevent – he replies that he does not. Gavroche tells the men the state of affairs outside their barricade – in effect, they are blocked.
Suddenly they are attacked from outside with grape-shot; two are killed. A tear trickles down Enjolras's face as he takes aim and kills the sergeant on the other side of the barricade.

Chapter 9

The insurgents know they must protect themselves from grape-shot. Mattresses are being used for the wounded. Enjolras orders Valjean to take up arms and he asks for a double-barrelled shotgun – he aims at ropes suspending a mattress on an upper floor where a woman had barricaded herself earlier. The mattress slips and falls to the street, outside the barricade. Valjean goes out into a hail of bullets and retrieves it. The mattress is put in place and protects them from the grape-shot.

Chapter 10

Cosette wakes at dawn that morning. She is confident Marius has received her letter and that they will be together again. She is certain she cannot live without him. She has no idea there are riots going on or that her father is not in the house.

Chapter 11

The soldiers continue firing on the barricade, but they do not fire back. They can see the head of someone in a helmet on a neighboring roof. Valjean takes aim and smashes the helmet – the soldier disappears. An officer replaces him and Valjean repeats his action. After this, there are no more spies on the roof.

Chapter 12

One of Enjolras's entourage wants to know why Valjean did not kill the roof-spies. Enjolras says Valjean achieves good by gun-shots alone.
Enjolras is disgusted when the soldiers kill their own by friendly-fire.

Chapter 13

As Paris comes to life that morning, some citizens begin to fire on the National Guard and the army. They are showing support for the insurgents. This delays the full scale attack on the barricade. The men behind the barricade are worn down and hungry.

Chapter 14

Courfeyrac and Bossuet find things to joke about as they face more grape-shot – they talk about how intrepid Enjolras is. Suddenly they face the barrage of more serious cannons. Balls mixed with grape-shot shower down upon them and damage the barricade. The insurgents open fire. Enjolras is worried they will run out of cartridges.

Chapter 15

Gavroche has gone outside the barricade and is taking the bullets of downed Guardsmen. Courfeyrac orders him back in but he runs off into the street, finding more bullets. He is obscured by the smoke of the spent artillery. He then begins teasing the enemy, singing and dodging bullets. Finally, he is hit, and falls, still singing. He is hit again, and dies.

Chapter 16

In the garden of the Luxembourg, two children are holding hands – two brothers, seven and five. They are hungry. The garden is deserted – the troops who had been there have gone to fight the insurgents. The boys are lost. They are the pair that Gavroche had shared his elephant with, his younger brothers. Normally they would not be allowed to be in the garden, but these are not normal times in Paris.

A middle-class man comes into the garden with his six year old son who is eating a pastry. He sees the boys and comments that standards are dropping. The boy does not want to finish his pastry and the man urges him to give it to the swans. They leave and the hungry boys grab the pastry out of the water.

Chapter 17

Marius and Combeferre dash to Gavroche's side but he is dead. Marius picks up the child and Combeferre grabs the bullets the boy had collected. He thought it ironic that Gavroche's father had saved his own but he could not save the boy.

A bullet grazes Marius's head and he is bandaged. The bullets are distributed to the insurgents. Valjean refuses to take any.

Chapter 18

It is noon. Enjolras orders half the men to take the paving stones and line the windowsills and roofs of the houses with them. He knows reinforcements have arrived outside. It is do-or-die time. The pub kitchen door is mailed shut. Valjean asks Enjolras if he may have the honor of killing Javert.

Chapter 19

Valjean is alone with Javert. He unties him and makes him get up, all the while holding a pistol. Javert's feet and hands are still bound and Valjean drags him outside, crossing the Mondetour barrier. Valjean reveals his identity and Javert tells him to take his revenge. Valjean frees him, astonishing the policeman, who leaves slowly. Valjean shoots his pistol, pretending to the others that he killed Javert. But Marius sees the man retreat and tells Enjolras. He now thinks Valjean is a spy too.

Chapters 20-21

The end had come for those behind the barricade. The army attacks the barriers and the assault is furious. Enjolras is at one end of the barrier and Marius at the other, the latter alone and unprotected, but he is in a dream-like state.
The barricade is attacked ten times, but still holds out; the men outnumbered sixty to one. Bossuet, Courfeyrac and Combeferre are all killed. The Corinthe is almost destroyed. Marius is injured but Enjolras has not been struck.

Chapter 22

Most of the barricade has given way. Some of the few remaining men try to escape through the houses around them. Enjolras and Marius run to protect the few remaining men and they manage to get inside the Corinthe and shut the army out – Enjolras is with them and Marius is outside. Marius, shot, begins to faint and is grabbed by another man.

Chapter 23

When the army breaks through into the Corinthe they find Enjolras alone on the third floor. They are overjoyed to have cornered the leader of the insurrection. He tells them to shoot him and twelve men take aim – the officer asks if he wants his eyes covered. Grantaire, meanwhile, has woken up from a deep drunken sleep. He offers to die with Enjolras and they are both shot. The soldiers go after the remaining insurgents.

Chapter 24

Marius has been taken prisoner by Valjean who has done little during the battle and has only minor injuries. The attack is now concentrated on the others – Valjean bears Marius off to a safer place but knows it is only a matter of time before they are found. He sees an iron grating in the ground – with the paving stones around it gone, it is easy to displace. He carries Marius down into the subterranean cavity.

Book 2

Chapters 1-6

A huge amount of sewage fills up the sewers and waterways around Paris every year. This is waste material; it could be used for manure, as the Chinese do. In London, too, the populace is being poisoned by the Thames. The sewer system in Paris has existed since medieval times. In the 19th century it is inadequate but the city has neither the will nor the resources to rectify the situation. Sometimes the sewer overflows and covers city streets. In the early 19th century a man named Bruneseau is employed to improve the sewer system and a good amount of the filth was cleaned out but the remnants of the old sewers are still disgusting.

By the time of Hugo's writing, the sewers are much improved. After Bruneseau was employed, more sewer lines were built. Six decades later, Paris has a system ten times bigger than it had been at the beginning of the century. In 1832 they were not as advanced, it took a cholera epidemic to improve things further. Much of the ancient system is still in place.

Book 3

Chapter 1

Valjean has disappeared with Marius – they are now sheltered from the hubbub overhead. He does not know if Marius is alive. He can see and hear nothing. He finds he can only walk a few paces. Soon his eyes adjust. He realizes the soldiers could come down here to search so time cannot be wasted. He advances with Marius, not knowing what other danger in the sewer might await them. He comes to a fork in the sewer – following the downward slope will take them to a populated area where it empties into the river Seine. He goes in the other direction, dragging Marius. They are in one of the most confusing parts of the sewer system. He walks for about half an hour, thinking he is reaching safety, when suddenly he realizes there are policemen behind him.

Chapter 2

Police had been sent in to search the sewers during the insurrection. Valjean's fear mounts when he sees them, but he has a better view than they have of him. Valjean stops and the police no longer hear him – they have a consultation and go off in a different direction. All Valjean knows is that their lanterns lights disappear and they are safe.

Chapter 3

Aboveground, one man is following another who seems to be staking out the banks of the Seine watching for any fugitives that might emerge from the sewers.

Chapter 4

It is becoming more difficult for Valjean to traverse the sewer system with Marius. Hunger and thirst are making it even more arduous and fatigue is setting in. He does not know if Marius is alive. He takes a route that ascends to the Seine – he knows they must get out soon. He comes to a place where he can lay Marius down and checks that he is still alive. He resumes his descent.

Chapter 5

There were areas in the Paris sewers which were like quicksand could take a person to their death. The less one carries, the less likely one is to die. These areas are known as "fontis".

Chapter 6
The fontis that Valjean encounters is due to the heavy rain of the day before. It is a pit of mire. He is soon into it up to his knees but cannot retreat. He goes in neck deep but finally it begins to recede.

Chapter 7
Valjean is now exhausted. He can only go a few steps at a time but then has a spurt of energy. Suddenly far away he sees daylight. He begins to almost run. When he reaches there he sees the opening is covered by grating, which is locked. It is now late evening. He lays Marius down and tries to dislodge the grating. He gives up in despair. He thinks only of Cosette.

Chapter 8
Suddenly a man appears before Valjean – it is Thenardier, who does not recognize him. He tells him he has the key to get out. He believes Valjean is a hired assassin and wants half of the payment Valjean would get or what Marius has in his pockets. Valjean shows him the money he has – it isn't much. Thenardier finds a small amount on Marius. He decides to take all the money and tells Valjean it is time to get out. He unlocks the grating and Valjean is now in the open air.

Chapter 9
Marius slides from Valjean's arms onto the shore. It is twilight. Valjean is enjoying the relief of being out of the sewer when he spots a man - Javert, who had been following Thenardier. Thenardier had an idea that Javert was following him so he uses Valjean as a ruse to get the policeman off his trail. Valjean identifies himself to Javert and tells him to arrest him. Javert asks who the man is that Valjean has been carrying but soon recognizes him from the barricade and remembers his name. They find the address of Marius's grandfather in his pocket and they load Marius into a carriage, and head to Gillenormand's.

Chapter 10

Marius is still alive; he is bleeding. When they reach his grandfather's, it is dark and everyone is asleep. The porter is told to fetch Marius's "father" – Javert tells the porter the young man is dead. Marius's aunt is woken up. Valjean and Javert leave without talking to her or M. Gillenormand. In the carriage Javert allows Valjean to send the carriage to his home address.

Chapter 11

Valjean wants to talk to Cosette, to tell her what has happened. He believes Javert will then arrest him. They arrive at his home and dismiss the carriage. Javert sends Valjean in alone. Upstairs he puts his head of the window and sees Javert has gone.

Chapter 12

Aunt Gillenormand is shocked to see Marius but soon doctor comes and he begins measures that will improve the young man's condition. Marius has many cuts, gashes, and a broken collar bone. He is apparently in shock, which is serious. He and the servants set to cleaning his wounds. Suddenly M. Gillenormand appears. He is shocked beyond speech. Finally though he begins to rant and accuses Marius of getting himself killed just to spite him. Gillenormand states it is time for him to die, too. Marius opens his eyes and looks at his grandfather – who faints.

<u>Book 4</u>

Chapter 1

Javert walks slowly away from Valjean's residence. He returns to the Seine where the rapids are. He stands there, thinking about his life. He does not know what to do about Valjean, whether to turn him in or let him go. Javert is not used to thinking and it pains him. He is embarrassed that a convict has treated him well. The code he lives by has been upset. He suddenly feels this should be left to God. In the end, Javert throws himself into the Seine.

Book 5

Chapter 1

Back in Montfermeil, the stonebreaker and road mender, Sieur Boulatruelle was still hoping to find Valjean's supposed buried treasure. He also knows Thenardier and his band of ruffians in the city; he had been in the apartment the day Valjean escaped from them. His drunkenness that day had saved him from being arrested. One day in the woods near Montfermeil sees a man in the distance who looks familiar. He doesn't know who it is but decides it is stranger and likely up to no good. He follows him but doesn't catch him – he comes upon a pick-axe and an empty hole.

Chapter 2

Marius is very ill as some of his wounds have become infected. He calls Cosette's name in his delirium. The doctor worries about his emotional state. Gillenormand sits nervously with Marius. Three months pass and finally he is on the mend and two more months of resting. Meanwhile any pursuit of him has cooled. His grandfather is overjoyed about his recovery and drives the doctor mad with his questions. Marius is consumed with thinking about Cosette.

Chapter 3

One day, when Marius has regained his strength, he tells his grandfather he wishes to marry. His grandfather agrees and tells him "an old gentleman" comes every day to see how Marius is doing, and Gillenormand has been making inquiries so knows all about Cosette. He agrees to let her come there that day.

Chapter 4

Cosette comes to see Marius with the whole household looking on. She makes an excellent impression upon Gillenormand. Cosette only wants to be alone with Marius but this will not happen. She comes in with Jean Valjean, well dressed in black and bearing a book wrapped in a package. Gillenormand tells Valjean he is giving permission for the marriage. He exhorts the others to talk so Marius and Cosette can have a private conversation. He then tells them there won't be any money for them after his death – Valjean opens his package and says there is over five hundred thousand francs for Cosette.

Chapter 5

Valjean had dug up his money from the forest near Montfermeil – the money he had removed from the bank when he left Montreuil-sur-Mer and buried with his candlesticks. Valjean now knows he is free from the threat of Javert; his body had been recovered from the Seine and this had been reported in the newspaper.

Chapter 6

The wedding is set for February. M. Gillenormand is half in love with Cosette himself. Valjean makes up a story about her ancestry, in case her illegitimacy becomes an impediment to the marriage. He claims she is the daughter of Fauchelevent of the convent and the nuns back him up. He says the money was a legacy from persons unknown to be inherited upon marriage.

Chapter 7

Valjean, known to the family as Fauchelevent, comes with Cosette every day. He does not reveal much of himself to Cosette's future family. Marius begins to wonder if he is the same man he saw at the barricade; he does not fully trust his memory from that time. He cannot believe his luck that he is still alive and happy. He and Valjean have a tacit agreement not to discuss the past.

Chapter 8

Marius feels he owes a debt of gratitude to two men – Thenardier and the mysterious stranger who brought him, injured, to his grandfather's. He wants to find them. He doesn't care that Thenardier, who saved his father's life, is a villain. Thenardier had been condemned to death and was now, in theory, a wanted man. Marius knows he was transported from the bank of the Seine to Gillenormand's – the coachman had testified to this.

Book 6

Chapter 1

Marius and Cosette marry on February 16th, 1833. Weddings were different then. People often had a reception at home, and the wedding party would witness the marital pair into their bedchamber. On the day they head to St. Paul's church, but must detour, due to the masquerade that marks Shrove Tuesday. At some point one of the revellers recognizes Jean Valjean riding in the wedding procession – it is Azelma Thenardier.

Chapter 2

Cosette is a beautiful bride and Marius a handsome groom. M. Gillenormand leads the bride into city hall and the church as Valjean has his arm in a sling. The ceremonies completed, they return to the carriages to go home. The bridal pair promise to each other they will return to the garden where they used to meet. At home crowds of people are waiting to greet them and the house is splendidly decorated, there is live music, and food. When they sit down to eat, Valjean has disappeared. His injured hand is bothering him. The reception goes well and the couple are blissfully happy as they consummate their marriage.

Chapter 3

When he left the reception Valjean returned home. He reflects that he will be here alone from now own – Toussaint had gone to be Cosette's maid. Valjean opens his valise that he had kept locked all these years – in it were the first clothes he had bought for Cosette at Montfermeil. All the memories come flooding back, and he falls on the bed, sobbing.

Chapter 4

Valjean's conscience is bothering him. He wants Cosette to be happy with Marius, but he, Valjean, has lost her. How was he now to relate to her? What part would he play in the couple's life? To let go completely is unthinkable. All night he agonizes.

Book 7

Chapter 1

Two days later Valjean goes to see the newlyweds. He asks the servant to tell Marius he would like to see him privately. Marius enters and calls Valjean "father", happy to see him. He reminds Valjean that there is a room there if he wants to move in. Marius prattles on until Valjean breaks in and tells him he is an ex-convict. He tells Marius he pretended to have an injured hand so that he could not sign as a witness at the wedding; he would have had to use a false name. He assures Marius he and Cosette are not blood relatives and that she was an orphan that he adopted. Marius asks why he did not just keep this a secret. Valjean replies that he is being honest. He goes on to say how he belongs to no-one, to no family. He struggled all night with his conscience. He adds that the authorities believe he is dead, but fears someone one day will recognize him.

Suddenly Cosette enters, thinking they are discussing politics. Marius says they are talking business and she will be bored. She tells Valjean to hug and kiss her, but soon senses something is wrong. Marius convinces her to leave and she pretends to be angry. Valjean begins to cry and says that he wishes he were dead. Marius offers him some money but tells him he cannot see Cosette again. Valjean knows he cannot do this and finally Marius agrees, saying he can come every evening.

Chapter 2

Since he had known Cosette, Marius had never warmed up to Valjean and now he is not surprised to find out about the man's background. He thinks he has been duped and is wondering about Cosette's background as well. He had conveniently ignored the incident at the Gorbeau hovel, when he saw Valjean confronted by Thenardier. Love had blinded him. He feels some compassion for Valjean and admiration for his honesty. He wonders why Valjean had appeared at the barricade for he had not taken up arms. He believes that perhaps he had come to avenge Javert. Valjean is repugnant to him now but what can he do? He would have to let him visit for Cosette's sake. Marius questions his wife about Valjean and she says only good of him.

Book 8

Chapter 1

The next evening Valjean goes to see Cosette. The room he waits in is not clean or well-kept. Valjean sits down and dozes off – he is both tired and hungry. Cosette appears and she is confused over the arrangement to meet her father here. She tells him he will dine with them, he refuses. He tells her not to call him "father", that she no longer needs one. She wants to know what is going on. He says his object in life was to make her happy and this has been accomplished. He leaves.

Chapter 2

Cosette has the room where she met her father cleaned up. Her father visits at the same time each day and Marius is absent when he arrives. The household gets used to Valjean's odd habits. Gillenormand simply says "he's an original", an eccentric. Cosette's only complaint during this time is that Toussaint does not get along with Nicolette, the Gillenormand servant. Marius is practicing law and the old grandfather is well.

Chapter 3

As time moves on, the relationship between Valjean and Cosette cools. She calls him "Monsieur Jean". He still visits for an hour each day.

One day in April Marius and Cosette visit the garden in Rue Plumet. Valjean comes to see Cosette that evening but she has not returned. He leaves but returns the next day. He asks why he has not replaced Toussaint, who has left, and why they do not have their own carriage. To himself he wonders if Marius is pinching pennies. Marius asks Cosette if she would be willing to live on his small income only. Valjean thinks Marius wonders about the origin of Valjean's money. One day when he visits Cosette, their armchairs in the downstairs room are gone. Valjean pretends he removed them. The next two evenings he does not visit and Cosette sends to find out where he is. He sends a reply that he is busy and that he is taking a trip soon.

Chapter 4

In the spring and summer of 1833 an elderly man walks the same route each morning but as the weeks pass his route is shorter and shorter. He appears exhausted and depressed. The locals think he is a little strange.

Book 9

Chapter 1

Being happy means one can forget one's sense of duty. Marius feels he has done the right thing in slowly estranging Valjean from Cosette. He still believes Valjean was a spy during the uprising. Cosette herself always does what her husband wants without giving it much thought, although she is still attached to Valjean and expresses worry. Overall though, her youth means she is more concerned with her life with Marius.

Chapter 2

There comes a day when Valjean does not leave his apartment and the next day, his bed. His portress prepares his meals but he stops eating. He sees no-one but her. The portress's husband thinks Valjean is dying. She gets a doctor to look at Valjean – he says the man is in good health but has a broken heart.

Chapter 3

One evening Valjean realizes his health is very bad. This motivates him to get up and get dressed. He opens his valise and removes the first clothing he bought for Cosette and spreads them on his bed. He lights two candles in the bishop's candlesticks. These actions fatigue him. In the mirror he looks eighty, only a year before he looked no more than fifty. He finds a pen, ink and paper and writes to Cosette. He explains how he came by the money he gave her, that he got it honestly as a businessman in Montreuil-sur-Mer He cries when he finishes, grieved that he will never see her again.

Chapter 4

That evening Marius receives a note from Thenardier, who is waiting for him in the antechamber. Cosette is in the garden with Gillenormand. The note says Thenardier has information that Marius could use to drive a certain person out of the house forever. Marius is overjoyed that he will meet Thenardier, who saved his father's life, at last. But it is not Thenardier but a man named Thenard, who wants to sell him a secret. He tells him Valjean is a thief and an assassin, an ex-convict. Marius replies that he knows this already. Marius accuses the man of being Thenardier (he is). Thenardier shows Marius a piece of his own jacket, which he claims was Valjean's (he took it from Marius after they had left the sewer). Marius pays Thenardier off so that he can go to Panama.

Marius goes to Cosette and tells her he has been a fool and a wretch; they take a carriage to Valjean's home. He explains what he has found out about Valjean; that the man is a hero and near-saint.

Chapter 5

Valjean is very ill but still breathing when Marius and Cosette arrive. He is overjoyed to see Cosette. She cries and calls him "father". He tells her he needed to see her to go on living and she chides him for his foolish and wicked behavior. He notices Marius and says he must have pardoned Valjean. Marius says that Valjean is an angel but why hadn't he told them the truth?

Valjean tells them he is dying. Cosette replies they are going to take him home, where he will live. The doctor arrives and Valjean introduces "his children". The doctor knows there is little hope and Valjean is accepting his imminent death. He tells them the money he has left is honest money. He dies peacefully.

Chapter 6

In the cemetery of Pere-Lachaise there is a stone, subject to the ravages of time. There is no name on the stone, as was the wish of the man buried there. It is the grave of Jean Valjean.

About BookCaps

We all need refreshers every now and then. Whether you are a student trying to cram for that big final, or someone just trying to understand a book more, BookCaps can help. We are a small, but growing company, and are adding titles every month.

Visit www.bookcaps.com to see more of our books, or contact us with any questions.

Made in the USA
Lexington, KY
11 March 2013